ARCHITECTURE IS A COLLECTIVE OCCUPATION,
A GROUP ENDEAVOUR THAT DRAWS ON THE
KNOWLEDGE AND INPUT OF A WIDE RANGE OF
PARTICIPANTS. RENZO PIANO HAS ALWAYS SOUGHT
TO COMPARE NOTES AND EXCHANGE IDEAS WITH
OTHER ARCHITECTS AND ENGINEERS, AS WELL AS
TAKING INTO ACCOUNT THE VIEWS OF CLIENTS
AND EXPERTS ON EACH AND EVERY PROJECT.
THE DECISION TO BEGIN THIS BOOK WITH A 'FAMILY
PHOTO ALBUM' IS A WAY OF ACKNOWLEDGING
THE TRAVELLING COMPANIONS WHO HAVE
GENEROUSLY SUPPORTED RENZO PIANO FROM
THE MID-1960s TO THE PRESENT DAY.
RIGHT: THE INITIAL GROUP OF COLLEAGUES WHO
WORKED WITH RENZO PIANO AT THE ERZELLI,
GENOA, IN THE LATE 1960s.

FLAVIO MARANO, AN ENGINEER
WHO TRAINED AT THE
UNIVERSITY OF GENOA, WAS
THE FIRST PERSON RECRUITED
BY RENZO PIANO, IN 1968.

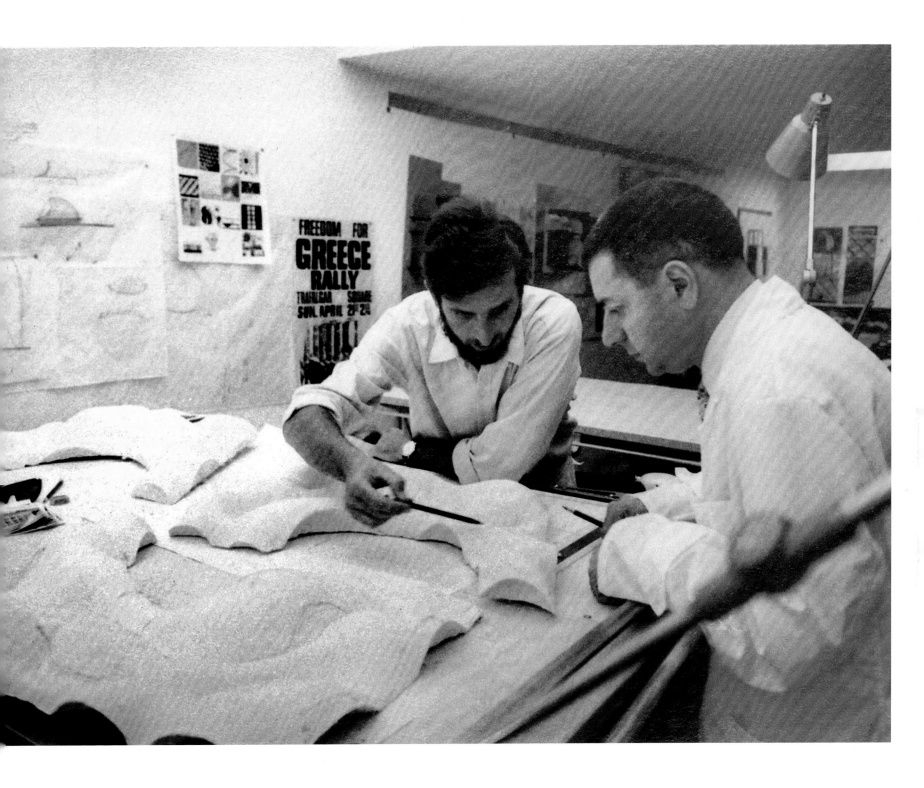

LEFT: SOME OF THE PIANO & ROGERS TEAM VISIT THE POMPIDOU CENTRE WORKSITE, 1972.

CENTRE: RICHARD AND SU ROGERS WITH RENZO PIANO. CLEARLY VISIBLE IN PROFILE, SHUNJI ISHIDA, AN EMPLOYEE FROM 1972 AND LATER A PARTNER OF RENZO PIANO BUILDING WORKSHOP (RPBW).

RIGHT: PETER RICE, RENZO PIANO AND RICHARD ROGERS SIT ASTRIDE A GERBERETTE AT THE POMPIDOU CENTRE WORKSITE, 1974.

LEFT: RENZO PIANO
AND RICHARD
ROGERS DURING
THE INAUGURATION
OF THE POMPIDOU
CENTRE, 1977.

RIGHT: NORIAKI
OKABE, RENZO
PIANO AND SHUNJI
ISHIDA WORK ON THE
MODELS, GENOA,
c. 1979.

LEFT: THE STUDIO IN VIALE MODUGNO, GENOA PEGLI, *c.* 1980. AS WELL AS RENZO PIANO, YOU CAN SEE ROSELLA BIONDO, MAGDA ARDUINO, ANGELA SACCO, RINALDO GAGGERO, OTTAVIO DI BLASI, SHUNJI ISHIDA, FRANÇOIS DORIA AND ALESSANDRO TRALDI.

RIGHT: THE STUDIO IN PARIS, IN THE RUE SAINTE-CROIX DE LA BRETONNERIE, *c.* 1980. TO THE RIGHT OF RENZO PIANO STANDS BERNARD PLATTNER, AN EMPLOYEE FROM 1973 AND LATER A PARTNER OF RPBW.

DURING THE 1980s THE STUDIO IN GENOA WAS LOCATED ON THE FIRST AND THIRD FLOORS OF A HISTORIC BUILDING IN PIAZZA SAN MATTEO. IN THE PHOTOGRAPHS, YOU CAN SEE A NUMBER OF YOUNG ARCHITECTS SUCH AS MARK CARROLL (A MEMBER OF THE PRACTICE FROM 1981), GIORGIO GRANDI (FROM 1984) AND GIORGIO BIANCHI (FROM 1985), LATER PARTNERS OF RPBW.

THE GENOA AND PARIS
TEAMS IN THE LATE 1980s AND
EARLY 1990s. ON THE LEFT
IS EMANUELA BAGLIETTO
(A MEMBER OF THE PRACTICE
FROM 1988), LATER A PARTNER
OF RPBW.

IN 1992 THE GENOA STAFF
MOVED TO THE NEW BUILDING
AT PUNTA NAVE. DESPITE THE
GRADUAL INTRODUCTION OF
COMPUTER TECHNOLOGY,
SKETCHING AND DRAWING
BY HAND – AND THE USE OF
MODELS – CONTINUED TO BE
ESSENTIAL WORKING METHODS.

BELOW: RPBW'S LONG-
SERVING MODEL-MAKER
DANTE CAVAGNA.

RIGHT: THE PUNTA NAVE
STUDIO, 2016.

LEFT: THE PARIS TEAM IN THEIR
PREMISES IN THE RUE SAINTE-CROIX DE
LA BRETONNERIE IN THE EARLY 1990s.

RIGHT: IN THE NEW HEADQUARTERS
IN THE RUE DES ARCHIVES, 2005. YOU
CAN MAKE OUT ANTOINE CHAAYA (A
MEMBER OF THE PRACTICE FROM 1987),
PHILIPPE GOUBET (FROM 1989) AND
JOOST MOOLHUIJZEN (FROM 1990), ALL
NOW PARTNERS OF RPBW.

DOUBLE PAGE OVERLEAF: THE
MODELLING WORKSHOP OF THE PARIS
STUDIO, OPENING DIRECTLY ONTO
THE STREET.

THE GENOA AND PARIS TEAMS
VISIT THE LONDON SHARD ON
RENZO PIANO'S SEVENTY-FIFTH
BIRTHDAY, 2012.

PREVIOUS DOUBLE PAGE:
THE ENTRANCE TO THE
PUNTA NAVE STUDIO, GENOA.

LEFT: RENZO PIANO WITH
PARTNER ELISABETTA
TREZZANI, A MEMBER OF
THE PRACTICE SINCE 1998.

RIGHT: A MEETING IS HELD
IN THE PARIS OFFICE; THE
MODELLING WORKSHOP AT
PUNTA NAVE, 2016.

RECENT PHOTOGRAPHS OF THE PARIS AND GENOA
TEAMS, INCLUDING THE YOUNGER GENERATION OF
PARTNERS: FRANCESCA BECCHI (FROM 2007), DANIELE
FRANCESCHIN (FROM 2009), ALBERT GIRALT (FROM
2009) AND LUIGI PRIANO (FROM 2011).

LORENZO CICCARELLI

Renzo Piano

& Renzo Piano Building Workshop

in cooperation with
the Renzo Piano
Foundation

LL

Quarto

This edition first published in 2023 by Frances Lincoln Publishing
an imprint of The Quarto Group.
One Triptych Place, London, SE1 9SH
United Kingdom
T (0)20 7700 6700
www.Quarto.com

This work is a joint initiative of the Renzo Piano Foundation and the Giunti Editore
publishing house.

The author would like to thank Renzo, Milly and Lia Piano, the archivists and staff of the
Renzo Piano Foundation, and all the Partners, architects and employees of the Renzo
Piano Building Workshop for their friendly assistance with the research and interviews
leading up to this publication.

A catalogue record for this book is available from the British Library.

ISBN 978-0-7112-8896-6
EBOOK ISBN 978-0-7112-8897-3

Front cover: © Michel Denancé
Back cover: © Renzo Piano Building Workshop
Translated by Simon Knight in association with First Edition Translations Ltd.
Cambridge, UK
Edited by David Price in association with First Edition Translations Ltd.
Cambridge, UK

10 9 8 7 6 5 4 3 2 1

Printed in China

'I like to think of the architect as someone who uses technology to create emotion.'
Renzo Piano

Introduction

Why a new book about Renzo Piano?

The curious reader can already consult his journal, in which the Genoese architect gives his own account of the human and professional aspects of the many adventurous projects he has completed in almost sixty years of activity, as well as a wealth of articles, books and exhibition catalogues in which some of the leading historians of contemporary architecture have discussed his work.[1]

Moreover, is a monograph, which inevitably focuses on the key player, the most effective medium for discussing an occupation that depends so heavily on exchanging ideas with the colleagues, consultants, clients and site managers required by every project – especially at the present time, when the aura surrounding the most prominent architects often conceals the digital and managerial complexity of the firms to which they lend their names?[2]

So I had doubts and reservations when the Giunti publishing house invited me to write this book, which above all is the sum of the possible answers I have tried to find to the above question. Certainly, its organization and critical approach reflect the conclusions I have reached.

Since 1964, the year in which he qualified as an architect, Renzo Piano and his colleagues have drawn up several hundred plans, many of which have been realized. I decided to deal with only a limited number of them, including some of the inevitable blockbusters, such as the Pompidou Centre (1971–1977), the Menil Collection (1981–1986), the Kansai Airport terminal (1988–1994), the reconstruction of the

Potsdamer Platz area (1992–2000), the Morgan Library (2000–2006) and the London Shard (2000–2012), while leaving aside other celebrated buildings, such as the Fondation Beyeler (1991–1997), the Jean-Marie Tjibaou Cultural Centre in Nouméa (1991–1998) and, more recently, the Whitney Museum of American Art in New York (2007–2015).[3] This selection – carefully considered and, of course, strictly personal – was based on precise criteria.

On the one hand, I opted for those projects, or those times, in which the evolution of Renzo Piano's architectural thinking and compositional strategies was most clearly illustrated. Instinctively rooted in worksite practice, he initially designed buildings characterized by the stringent integration of form, structure and services – buildings often very basic in their volumes and layout, but elegantly interpreting the lexicon, tools and craftsmanship of the 'first machine age'.[4] Subsequently, Piano applied this constructional expertise and experimental emphasis to the contexts of the historic European city and American conurbations, with the primary objective of preserving (where possible) or fostering (where necessary) the life and vitality of these places – designing buildings of sophisticated sobriety, blurring as much as possible the borderline between public and private space.[5]

On the other hand, I thought it necessary to discuss those commissions in which the fundamental role played by Piano's clients, consultants and many of his colleagues was most evident, and those occasions when the professional organizations he presided over[6] were obliged to deviate from his plans. It is a methodological imperative to give due emphasis to the collective dimension of the architectural profession at a time when, on the contrary, the media focuses on the 'archistar' phenomenon and imposes on distracted observers a one-sided 'artistic' interpretation.[7] I hope these initial comments will clarify the structure and content of this book.

Renzo Piano's formative years – his 'prehistory' – and the experimental structures he built between 1964 and 1970 illustrate to the highest degree the *cultura del fare* (hands-on culture) he always claimed to espouse. Free of the obligations and limitations imposed by clients, and from having to manage a large office, in those years Piano happily experimented with materials, assembly techniques, the use of models and the challenges of lightweight construction – these being the components of a legacy that continues to be influential.

His unexpected victory in the international competition to design the Pompidou Centre (also known as 'Beaubourg') tore the young architect away from this domestic setting, catapulting him and Richard Rogers (1933–2021) into the international limelight, to undertake an operation of long duration and enormous complexity. More than forty years on from the eye-catching architecture of the Parisian cultural centre, it can be seen as an exceptional and unrepeatable event in Piano's career. A product of the revolutionary cultural and social climate of 1968, Beaubourg should, in my opinion, be interpreted more as the outcome of Piano's experimentation up to that point than as anticipating his subsequent work.[8] The legacy of that experience was rather his friendship with Richard Rogers, his meeting with Shunji Ishida (b. 1944) and Bernard Plattner (b. 1946) – two young architects who turned out to be the pillars of the Genoa- and Paris-based offices of the Building Workshop – and his hitting it off with Peter Rice (1935–1992), the brilliant Irish engineer who played such a key role in the most highly regarded buildings that Piano designed in the years that followed.

The period between the inauguration of the Pompidou Centre in 1977 and his commission for the Menil Collection in 1981 was marked by Piano's return to Italy, along with a drastic reduction in the number of his colleagues and ever-closer human and professional synergy with Peter Rice, and, in particular, the launch in 1979 of the experiment with District Workshops (Laboratori di Quartiere), as commissioned by UNESCO. This was the first time that Piano had formulated strategies for intervention in established urban settings.

I see this period as his 'wilderness years'. Out of the limelight of the Pompidou Centre, which had brought him international fame, Piano had to make a fresh start, returning to the western suburb of Genoa from which he had come, and working on hybrid projects combining product design, experimentation with construction systems and small-scale architecture. His next great opportunity came in the late 1980s, when the collector Dominique de Menil (1908–1997) contacted Piano and entrusted him with the construction of a new museum in Houston. While the Pompidou Centre is still the building the public associates with Piano, in my opinion the Menil Collection was the real turning point in his career and is probably his masterpiece.

In his *Treatise on Architecture* (1465), Filarete stated that the successful outcome of a building project is due in equal measure to the client and the architect, regarded respectively as the father and the mother of the work.[9] And few works of the modern era confirm this assertion as clearly as the Menil Collection. We shall see how the dialogue between Dominique de Menil and Renzo Piano, and the latter's capacity to receive and give real substance to the Franco-American collector's views, resulted in a profound change in his public profile, accounting for much of the success that smiled on him in the following decades, especially in the United States.[10]

The numerical growth and managerial arrangements that characterize the recent output of the Renzo Piano Building Workshop are due above all to two major projects that dominated the 1990s: the Kansai International Airport terminal in Osaka and the reconstruction of the Potsdamer Platz area in Berlin. Discussing them together, in the same chapter, is a good way of explaining the transition I referred to at the beginning of this introduction: whereas the Osaka project can be interpreted as the most extreme and accomplished outcome of architecture understood as the 'art and technology of building', the Berlin project represents the most ambitious and masterly urban development performed by Piano and his co-workers.[11] The modelling of voids – the creation of public space – is precisely the aspect I have chosen to emphasize in the array of projects undertaken by the Building Workshop in the late 1980s and early 2000s, as it extended its field of action from Italy to the United States, launching out from the docks of Genoa's Porto Vecchio (1985–2001) to put in at Atlanta's High Museum of Art (1999–2005) and finally make landfall in New York with the extension to the Morgan Library.

The (positive) tension between the personal and collective dimensions of the architectural profession at the present time is one of the key aspects of this work, investigated by selecting and analysing a number of works and exploring the cooperation between Renzo Piano and the many colleagues, consultants and friends who have accompanied him on his journey. This tension has gradually increased in recent Building Workshop projects, which have been characterized by the creative and managerial inputs of the Partners and other associates of the practice.[12] In the final chapter of the book, my description of the organization and planning method of the Renzo Piano Building Workshop is based on an analysis of five projects. Three of these – the London Shard (2000–2012), the cultural centre of the Stavros Niarchos Foundation in Athens (2008–2016) and the City Gate project and the new Parliament building in Valletta (2009–2015) – are large-scale urban developments, products of a concerted effort by the practice's brightest talents. The other two – the Park Auditorium in L'Aquila (2010–2012) and the Emergency Paediatric Hospital in Entebbe, Uganda (2013–2020) – are rather design experiments conducted by Piano in a more intimate and personal way, drawing on the strengths of the Building Workshop but looking outwards to a greater extent and involving longstanding friends and colleagues. This rigorous selection of works, referenced to illustrate some clearly defined areas of research, is the strategy I have adopted in trying to produce a book that I hope will add a significant piece to the vast bibliographical jigsaw depicting Renzo Piano. Let the reader be my judge.

I have also interpreted the Giunti publishing house's invitation as an opportunity to revisit the vast panoply of research and writings I have devoted to Renzo Piano and the Building Workshop over the last decade. So, over the last two years I have supplemented my periods of study in the archives of the Renzo Piano Foundation since 2013 with a series of meetings and interviews with the Fellows, Partners and associates of the Building Workshop. The oral testimony of these key witnesses has added to and enriched the evidence of the drawings and documentation.

[1] Renzo Piano, *Giornale di bordo*, Passigli, Florence 1997 (first edition), 2005 (second edition), 2016 (third edition, written in conjunction with the Renzo Piano Foundation). For what I consider to be the most important bibliographical sources, see the notes at the end of each of the following chapters.

[2] See Lorenzo Ciccarelli, Sara Lombardi, Lorenzo Mingardi (eds.). *Largest Architectural Firms*. Design Authorship and Organization Management, Edifir, Florence 2021.

[3] The painful need to exclude these projects has been mitigated by the fact that there is a vast bibliography devoted to them, starting with the Renzo Piano Foundation's own series of monographs.

[4] Reyner Banham, author of the celebrated work *Theory and Design of the First Machine Age*, Architectural Press, London 1960, was one of the critics who paid the closest attention to Piano's work, helping to ensure his success in the British and American cultural context of the 1980s. See in particular Reyner Banham, 'Making Architecture: The High Craft of Renzo Piano', in Renzo Piano Building Workshop: 1964–1988', in *a+u*, 3, 1989.

[5] More than from Piano's Journal, this evolution is apparent from the pages of Peter Buchanan, *Renzo Piano Building Workshop: Complete Works*, vols. 1–5, Phaidon, London, 1993–2009. See also Paul Goldberg, *Renzo Piano and Building Workshop. Building and Projects* 1971-1989, Rizzoli, New York, pp. 7–9.

[6] Renzo Piano Architect from 1964; Piano & Rogers from 1971 to 1977; Atelier Piano & Rice from 1977 to 1981; and subsequently RPBW.

[7] Silvia Micheli, Gabriella Lo Ricco, *Lo spettacolo dell'architettura. Profilo dell'archistar*, Bruno Mondadori, Milan 2003. Though belonging, despite himself, to the rarefied group of celebrated 'archistars', Piano has always opposed the stylistic and subjective interpretation of his profession. See for example his comments in 'Il mestiere dell'architetto', in Renzo Piano, *Giornale di bordo*, Passigli, Florence 1997, pp. 10–19.

[8] An argument that I have explored in Lorenzo Ciccarelli, *Renzo Piano prima di Renzo Piano, I maestri e gli esordi*, Quodlibet/ Renzo Piano Foundation, Macerata 2017.

[9] Antonio Averlino aka Filarete, *Trattato di Architettura*, Il Polifilo, Milan 1972.

[10] Federico Bucci, 'In the Age of Piano', in *Casabella*, 797, 2011, pp. 69–70.

[11] See Luis Fernández-Galiano, 'Human Colour', in *Renzo Piano: The Art of Making Buildings*, Royal Academy of Arts, London 2018, pp. 145–149.

[12] The managerial structure of Partners and associate architects in the RPBW was established in 1997 and has been updated several times. The present Partners are Renzo Piano (b. 1937), Emanuela Baglietto (b. 1960), Francesca Becchi (b. 1978), Giorgio Bianchi (b. 1957), Mark Carroll (b. 1956), Antoine Chaaya (b. 1960), Daniele Franceschin (b. 1981), Albert Giralt (b. 1980), Philippe Goubet (b. 1964, Managing Director), Joost Moolhuijzen (b. 1960), Luigi Priano (b. 1983) and Elisabetta Trezzani (b. 1968).

18.00

Particolare A

Sezione sulle piramidi.

20.00

20.12

Sezione sulle travi di
pevimetro

Particolare D

Sezione sull'accoppiamento
piramide e vetrata di ingresso

Sezione sulle travi di perimetro

Particolare B

19.80

12

B

E

F

Pezzoni quadro estruso

D

2.00

10

20.00

2.00

4.00

4.06

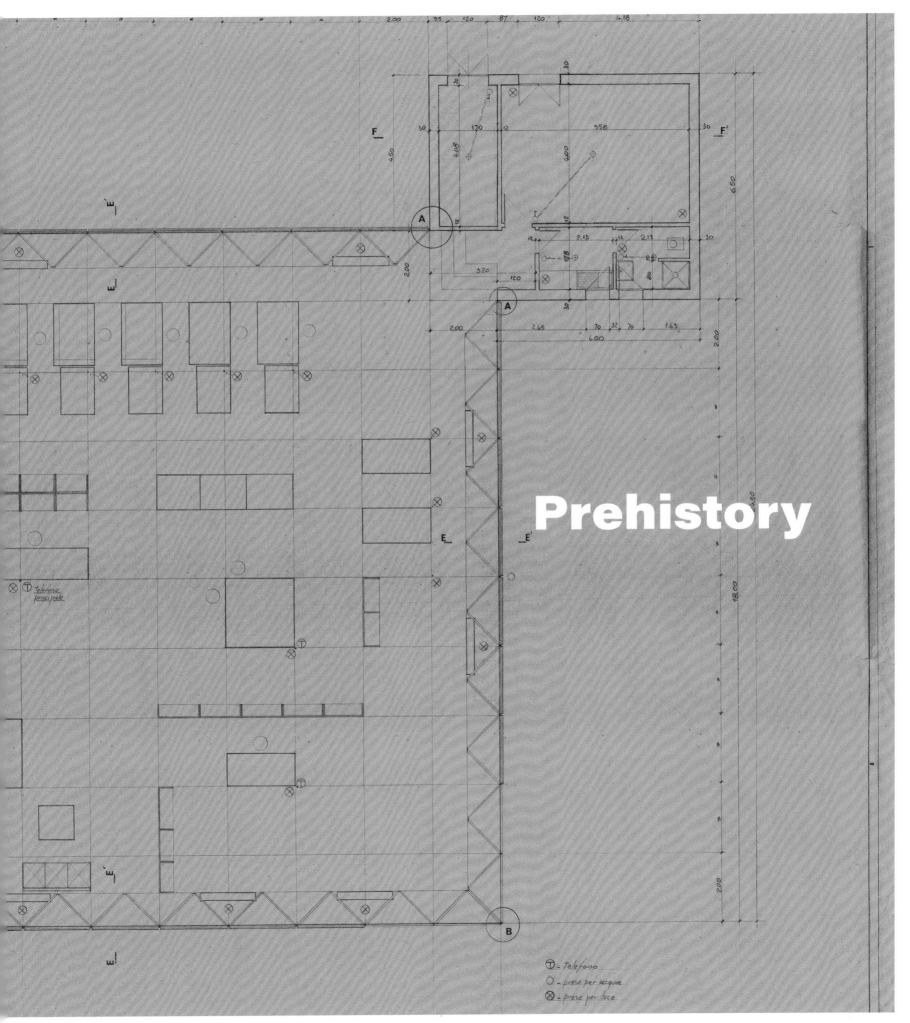

Prehistory

Renzo Piano likes to define his apprenticeship years – the period from when he joined the Faculty of Architecture in Florence in 1958 to when he won the Pompidou Centre commission in 1971 – as 'my prehistory'.[1] While the history of the Genoa-born architect (at least for the media) begins with Beaubourg – the building that won him international acclaim and forty years later still typifies him in the eyes of the general public – his earlier work is by no means unimportant. Unlike many modern architects, who have tried to remove their youthful activities from the official narrative of their work, Piano has always emphasized the importance of the work he did immediately after graduating, especially with regard to his methods.

Nothing of what Piano created in those early years has survived the march of time: the delicate canopies, prefabricated roof structures, industrial hangars, service stations and exhibition pavilions constructed by the young architect have all deteriorated over the years, been damaged and, finally, been destroyed.[2] And that was the original intention. They were not architectural trial-pieces but exercises in construction, not permanent works but flexible contrivances, made up of parts that could be assembled and dismantled. Still free of financial and managerial constraints, and of clients' demands, the products of this prehistory are the purest distillation of the sources of Renzo Piano's architecture, and it is in this that their interest lies. Experiments in construction that only later were to bear offspring, they contain in embryo various aspects of the architectural programme that was to characterize not only the Pompidou Centre but many of the Building Workshop's masterpieces: the primacy of construction and building site; the stringent integration of form, structure and services; a fascination with the ever-changing gradations of natural light; the predominance of the roof over the infilling of front, back and sides.

Piano was born in 1937 in Pegli, a seafaring district in Genoa's western suburbs.[3] In 1958, he enrolled with the Faculty of Architecture in Florence but left two years later and moved to the Milan Polytechnic, where in 1964 he completed his studies defending a thesis on modular coordination in discussion with Giuseppe Ciribini (1913–1990), at that time a leading expert on prefabricated buildings and construction technologies.[4] From 1960 to 1962, he also worked as an apprentice in the studio of Franco Albini (1905–1977) and, after graduating, between 1965 and 1967, as assistant to Marco Zanuso (1916–2001) on the course covering the morphology and processing of materials at the Milan Polytechnic.[5] In the years during which Italian architectural culture was gaining international recognition, thanks to a combination of political militancy, historical/urban analysis and architectural planning – and Milan was one of the centres of this movement – Piano chose to devote himself to building techniques, to experimentation with plastics and prefabricated construction.[6] This was a decision that was natural and instinctive rather than carefully considered, determined above all by his personal history and background.

Renzo Piano has building in his blood. His father Carlo (1892–1973) had established a small-scale construction business in the 1930s. This business grew in the post-war years, driven by the economic recovery of Genoa and the demand for new housing. Its premises were on the Erzilli Hill, in the heart of the city's industrial district, a couple of miles from the Ansaldo engineering works, the Italsider steelworks, the industrial port and the airport runways.[7] Construction site machinery, concrete, brick walls and the 'magic' of building work are some of Piano's most vivid childhood memories, making an indelible impression on his later career as an architect.[8]

In the mid-1960s, when Piano graduated and gained his professional qualification, management of the family business passed to his older brother Ermanno (1928–1991), a key figure in the young architect's developing career.[9] Practically all the projects of Renzo Piano's 'prehistory' were commissions obtained by the Impresa Piano Ermanno,

ERMANNO PIANO WALKING ON THE ROOF OF HIS BROTHER RENZO'S EXPERIMENTAL STUDIO. IN THE BACKGROUND, ERZELLI HILL AND THE WESTERN OUTSKIRTS OF GENOA, 1969.

which Ermanno then entrusted to his younger brother, even though he could have relied on his own technical department. And it was with equipment belonging to the family business, and employing the family workforce, that Renzo was able to build his first experimental structures and small pavilions, developing under the benevolent eye of his brother the 'hands-on culture' that he was to point to as his defining characteristic in the decades that followed.[10]

▶ The first project completed by Piano, in 1965, was a small factory building for a sawmill at Ceranesi, in the hinterland of Genoa.[11] He designed a tunnel vault 25 metres long and 18 metres wide, with a central height of just over 6 metres. It was to be assembled in eighteen days by four workers, using only a bridge crane. For his material, Piano decided to use galvanized iron, which was cheap and could be processed using the press and cutter already owned by the family business.

As with all these early projects, Piano did not focus on the arrangement of volumes or internal layout – a simple undivided area – but rather on the design of a *pezzo* (a key component) and the way a number of these components (*pezzi*) were to be assembled.[12] With all types of cladding ruled out, the shell of the building ideally had to result from the mass production and assembly of these *pezzi*, as a result of which the structural requirements and labour involved were reduced to a minimum.

Two triangular pieces of galvanized iron were welded together to make a rhomboid-shaped component with a stiffening fold along the main axis. Each of these components, weighing 25 kilograms, was constructed in the Impresa Piano Ermanno factory and delivered to the construction site with holes pre-drilled in their lateral flanges for assembly with steel bolts, and a neoprene joint to make them watertight. The vault, consisting of four hundred of these rhomboid-shaped *pezzi*, was supported on two low reinforced concrete walls, while modules with glazed, openable windows, located in the ceiling of the vault and at its base, ensured the lighting and ventilation of the internal space. Polystyrene panels applied to the internal surfaces of the galvanized iron rhomboids provided insulation, while two non-load-bearing brick walls closed off the ends of the vault.[13]

Piano's response to his first commission was a unique, unrepeatable building, but with an open-ended prefabrication system based on the development of a *pezzo* that would meet the needs of form and structure. It was no coincidence that, a year later, the same system was re-employed to construct a similar vault made of reinforced-polyester rhomboidal elements to roof over the sulphur-extraction quarries at Pomezia.[14] Not an artist's proof but rather the fallible experiment of a craftsman builder.

A YOUTHFUL RENZO PIANO
OVERSEES THE ASSEMBLY OF
ONE OF HIS EARLY LIGHTWEIGHT
STRUCTURES MADE OF
REINFORCED POLYESTER
COMPONENTS, PRODUCED TO HIS
OWN DESIGN AND ASSEMBLED
BY WORKERS FROM THE FAMILY
BUSINESS AT THE ERZELLI, GENOA,
IN 1965.

In Piano's 'prehistory' we can identify the future markers of his career as an architect: his affinity with building site practice, a rational approach to space, attention to building materials and the construction process, the centrality of roofing structures and a predilection for the light and airy.

Piano was attracted by the potential of so-called 'structural prefabrication', as codified by Pier Luigi Nervi (1891–1979). A comparison of the Ceranesi building and the aircraft hangars at Orvieto (1939–1941) reveals striking similarities – a way of bridging the gap between conception and construction, between drawing board and worksite.[15] As is well known, Nervi would break down the shell of a building into a number of lightweight components of limited size, reduced to a few standard shapes, that could be mass-produced in his workshop and welded on site.[16] This method required a well-trained workforce with perfect mastery of the construction techniques adopted by the designer, and for this both Nervi and Piano could rely on family construction businesses. Although Piano focused on the use of plastic materials, rather than reinforced concrete, Nervi and his construction projects were a fundamental, never-surpassed model for the young architect. Nervi was an engineer, but in Piano's eyes he was above all a *baumeister* – a master builder – with whom he instinctively sensed an affinity.[17]

Another *baumeister* to whom Piano looked for inspiration was undoubtedly Jean Prouvé (1901–1984), whom the young architect sought out in Paris in 1965, attending some of the lectures Prouvé gave at the Conservatoire National des Arts et Métiers.[18] In studying his elegant buildings with prefabricated components – the Maisons de

THE STRUCTURE OF THE SAWMILL
BUILDING AT CERANESI WAS
DETERMINED BY PIANO'S DESIGN OF
THE KEY COMPONENT (THE *PEZZO*)
AND BY HIS DRY ASSEMBLY METHOD.
PREFABRICATION, LIGHTNESS,
INTEGRATION OF FORM AND
STRUCTURE: THE STATEMENT OF A
PROGRAMME TO WHICH PIANO WAS
TO REMAIN LOYAL THROUGHOUT THE
YEARS TO COME.

Meudon (1950–1951), the school at Vantoux (1950) or the Maison des Jours Meilleurs (1954) – Piano must have immediately recognized the principles he was pursuing in his early construction projects: lightweight prefabrication, the aesthetic value of elegant joining elements and the building site as a dry-assembly workshop.[19] Prouvé was for Piano above all a *plieur des tôles*, a virtuoso craftsman able to handle and fold sheet metal. More than a design artist, he was 'a workshop man, expert in every forging technique, master of the skills required to work with metals'.[20]

In his early construction projects, Piano followed in the footsteps of Nervi and Prouvé:

getting his spark of inspiration from experimentation with his materials and ways of using them in prefabrication; organizing the construction site as a dry-assembly workshop; and aiming for elegance and 'poetry' in designing the *pezzo* on which the structure and the way of joining it all together was based.[21] And until the Beaubourg commission, Piano sought to advance this programme using plastics – then the avant-garde materials in the construction industry, above all reinforced polyester, which was the more robust because of the glass fibres forming a continuous mesh within it.[22]

THE FACTORY BUILDING FOR THE
FAMILY BUSINESS AT THE ERZELLI,
GENOA, 1966–1968, WAS CONCEIVED
BY PIANO AS AN OPEN-ENDED
PREFABRICATED SYSTEM, WITH A
METAL STRUCTURE AND A ROOF
OF TRANSLUCENT REINFORCED
POLYESTER.

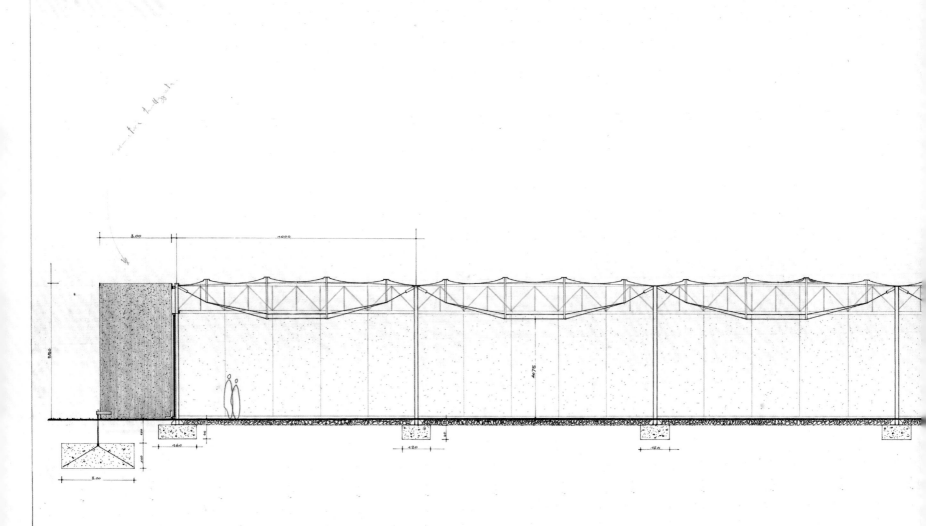

THE PREMISES OF THE FAMILY BUSINESS
WERE ALSO THE LABORATORY IN
WHICH PIANO EXPERIMENTED WITH
CONSTRUCTION TECHNIQUES IN THE
EARLY PART OF HIS CAREER, FOR EXAMPLE
IN DESIGNING THE COMPONENTS OF THE
ITALIAN PAVILION OF INDUSTRY FOR THE
1970 OSAKA EXPOSITION (SEE BELOW).

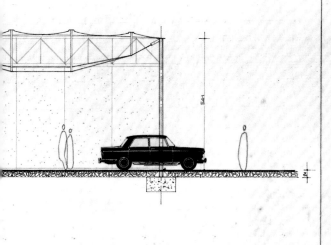

Dott. Arch. RENZO PIANO

2 MAG. 1967

1:50

SEZIONE

66 OFF 243.

OFF_E_001

▶ Having established his programme of work, Piano began organizing the professional structure that would support it effectively: more an experimentation and production workshop than a conventional architectural practice.[23] In 1968 he recruited an engineer, Flavio Marano (b. 1933), trained in the Faculty of Engineering in Genoa, where he had attended the design courses of Luigi Carlo Daneri, 'one of those architects who gets his hands dirty on site', and Giorgio Fascioli, a surveyor with expertise in designing doors and windows. He also took on some part-time employees.[24]

The establishment of this first multidisciplinary professional organization, however minimal, enabled Piano to take time off from the day-to-day activity of the studio – generously supplied with projects by the Impresa Piano Ermanno – and devote himself to developing new experimental structures, not at the drawing board but using studio models, trying them out immediately and putting them into production in the family factory. For this reason, his studio needed to be close to the Impresa Piano Ermanno factory, and in just a few months the young architect designed both a new factory for the business (1966–1968) and new premises for his studio (1968–1969), one adjacent to the other on the Erzelli Hill.[25]

It was Ermanno again who commissioned his brother to design the warehouse building in which the company's materials and equipment were to be kept. As usual, Piano took advantage of the freedom granted him to design not so much a building as an open-ended construction system of prefabricated components. The building was a complex structure, in which robust concrete panels on either side acted as counterweights to a system of steel tie-rods and

THE CALCULATED LIGHTNESS OF THE ROOF OF THE IMPRESA PIANO ERMANNO FACTORY WAS THE RESULT OF A SOPHISTICATED STRUCTURAL SYSTEM OF METAL UPRIGHTS AND CABLES, COUNTERBALANCED BY HEAVY SIDE PANELS AND BURIED BLOCKS OF CONCRETE.

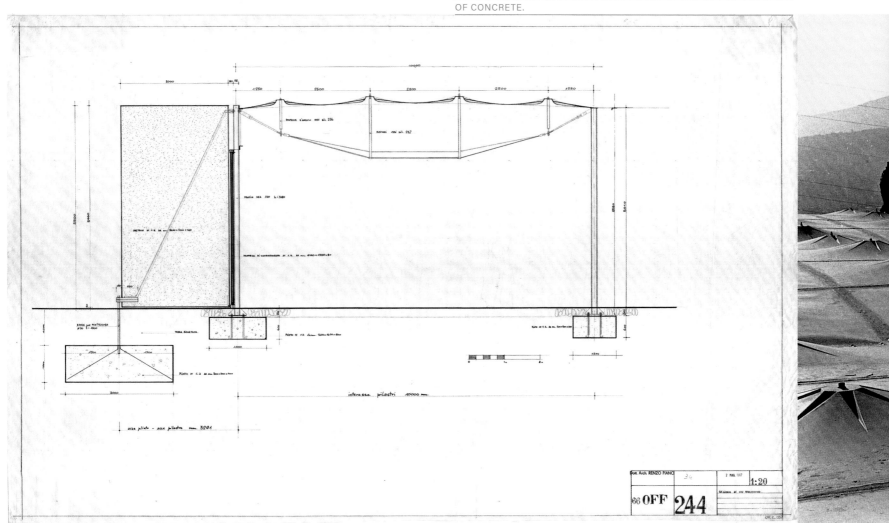

struts holding up the translucent reinforced polyester roof.[26]

The poor elasticity modulus of plastic materials was the most serious impediment to their use in construction work. This was a problem to which the German engineer Frei Otto (1925–2015) had found a brilliant solution: prestressing the material and inducing a distribution of forces in the membrane contrary to the force generated by loading the structure.[27] Under stress, the reinforced polyester membrane stiffened, with the result that it had the necessary elasticity to absorb accidental loads and gusts of wind.

ATTENTION TO DETAIL IN DESIGN IS ONE OF THE KEY FEATURES OF RENZO PIANO'S ARCHITECTURAL WORK. THE IMPRESA PIANO ERMANNO FACTORY WAS NO EXCEPTION, AS EVIDENCED BY THE STAR-SHAPED CORRUGATIONS JOINING THE METAL STRUTS TO THE REINFORCED POLYESTER ROOF PANELS.

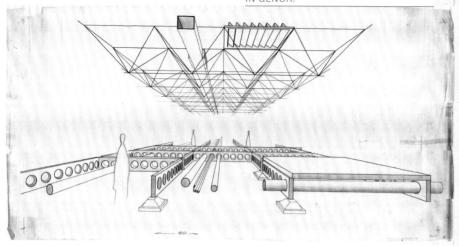

Once again Piano applied himself to the design of a *pezzo*, the basic module of his construction system: a roof panel, 2.5 metres square, composed of two chemically welded sheets of reinforced polyester. In the centre of the panel a star-shaped radial corrugation gripped a steel reinforcing plate embedded in the plastic. This plate absorbed the thrust from the strut beneath it. The stress was transferred through the star-shaped corrugation to the surface of the panel, causing it to stiffen.[28] Sixteen modular components were produced on site at the Erzelli. Bonded together with polymeric resins, they made up the 10-metre-square modules that formed the roof of the building. Given the light weight of polyester, these modules could be lifted by a crane and delicately placed on the structure that would support and put them under stress, consisting of a framework of steel uprights 5.4 metres in height. These uprights, resting on prefabricated reinforced-concrete plinths, were arranged in a 10-metre-square mesh pattern, so that each roof module was held up by four supports.

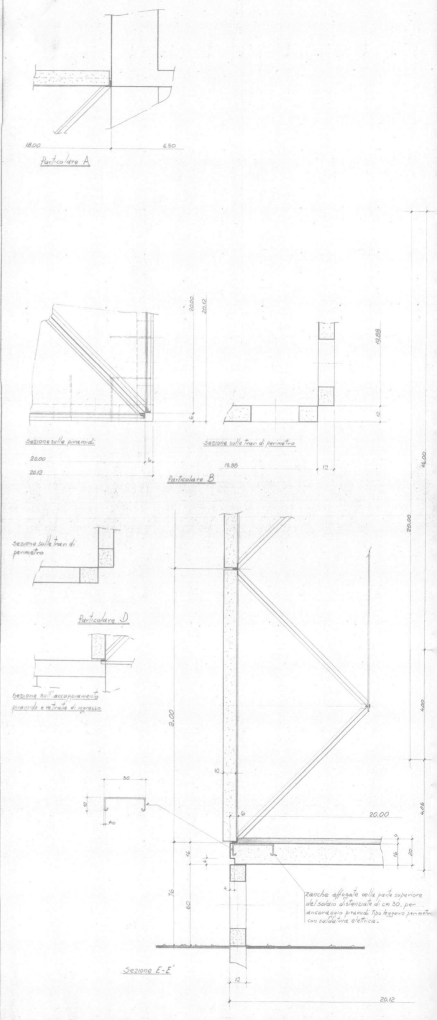

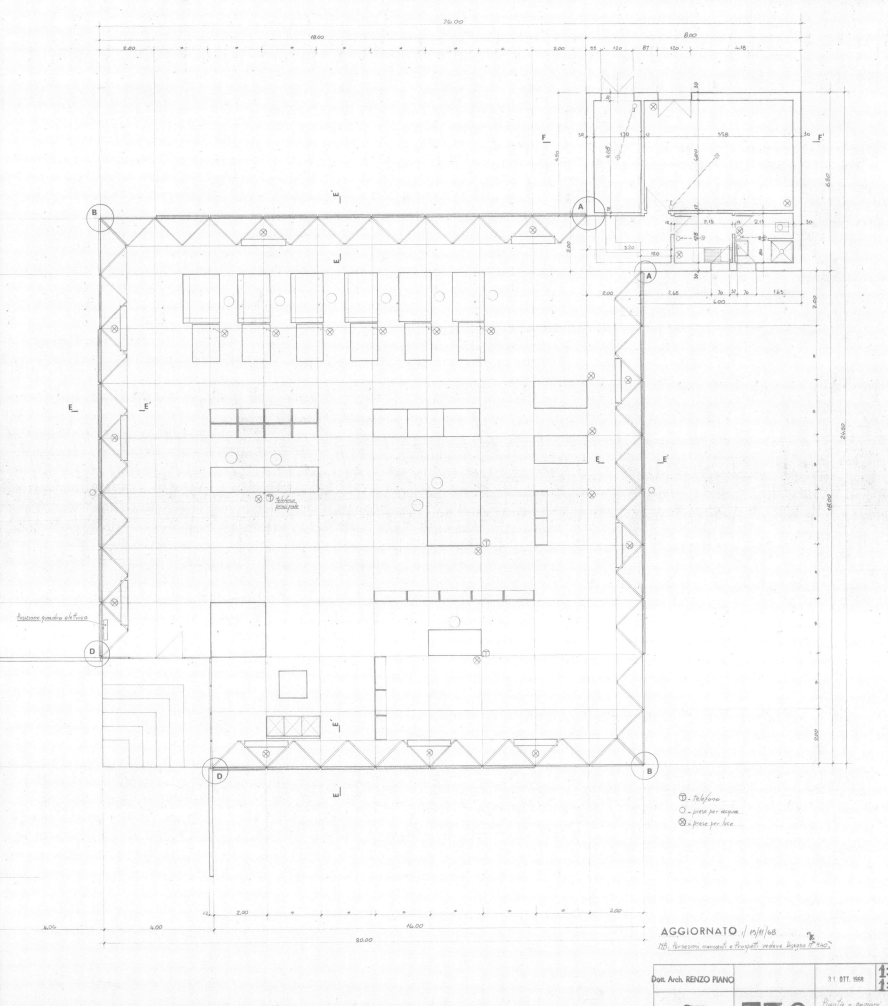

⊕ - telefono
○ - presa per acqua
⊗ - prese per luce

Posizione quadro elettrico

AGGIORNATO il 15/11/68

NB. Per sezioni mancanti e Prospetti vedere Disegno N° 540.

Dott. Arch. RENZO PIANO

31 OTT. 1968

1:10
1:50

68 ST

539

Pianta e sezioni
locali studio tecnico.

EVERY COMPONENT OF THIS BUILDING WAS
DESIGNED FOR PREFABRICATION AND DRY
ASSEMBLY, AGAIN WITH THE VITAL CONTRIBUTION
OF EQUIPMENT AND LABOUR FROM THE NEARBY
FAMILY BUSINESS.

HERE AGAIN, THE STYLISTIC CHARACTER
OF THE BUILDING WAS DETERMINED BY A
PREFABRICATED ROOF PANEL: A DOUBLE
SHEET OF REINFORCED POLYESTER
DESIGNED TO ADMIT LIGHT ONLY FROM
A NORTHERLY DIRECTION.

Between these, via connecting plates, was stretched a network of six spiral-strand cables, to which were attached the sixteen struts. Once a roof unit was lowered onto this support, each strut was bolted to the reinforcing plate of each reinforced polyester panel. The network of cables was then tensioned by acting on the turnbuckles located between the uprights and the connecting plates. The reinforced polyester membranes, initially flexible, were then stiffened by the force of the chain reaction exerted by the struts.

In the summer of 1968, Impresa Piano built its own factory to a rectangular plan 60 x 40 metres, one of the many spatial solutions possible using the open-ended system. However, this elegant construction lacked one final component. The accumulated stresses of the roof structure needed to be discharged to the ground. Passing from frame to frame, they accumulated in the twenty uprights around the perimeter. To each of them, Piano bolted a strong prefabricated panel of reinforced concrete which, traversed diagonally by a steel tie-bar, was connected to a 9-cubic-metre plinth, also of reinforced concrete: two formidable counterweights. Having balanced the structure, Piano enclosed the building with prefabricated lightweight concrete panels, bolted to the uprights.

One of the characteristics of reinforced polyester that most fasci-nated Piano was its translucid quality, allowing the passage of roughly 30 per cent of solar radiation and thus illuminating the workspace with natural light without the need for other systems, at least in the hours of daylight. The ability to use natural light, and to design roofs that admit just the right amount – an aspect of the most celebrated works of the mature period of the Renzo Piano Building Workshop[29] – was already evident in these early projects, as is clear in the office building that Piano built in 1969 in the vicinity of the family factory at the Erzelli.[30]

The small building was divided into two parts: to the larger volume, 20 metres square, was connected a reinforced concrete cube containing the services. The components 'kit' consisted of foundation beams of pre-compressed concrete; pyramids of steel sections; wall panels of light concrete and expanded polyurethane; and translucid roofing panels in reinforced polyester. The foundation beams on which the structure was to stand, with holes drilled in them and a ventilated cavity, were small and light enough to be handled by two workmen. The structural component – the same for the side walls and the roof – was simply a steel pyramid, 2 metres square at the base and 1 metre high.

Manoeuvred and lowered into place by a crane, the pyramids were bolted to one another. Traversed by the ducting for the air-conditioning, lighting and fire-fighting systems, they supported the roofing panels. The prefabricated side-wall component, triangular in shape and 10 centimetres thick, was a sandwich of expanded polyurethane between two layers of light reinforced concrete. The panels, which could be easily replaced for maintenance purposes, fitted into grooves in the metal sections of the structural pyramids and were secured with bolts. The north-light roof of reinforced polyester had an opaque finish for the south-facing sections and a translucid finish for the north-facing ones, so that only the steady, indirect light from the north filtered through into the workspace beneath. The same solution, albeit in different forms, was later adopted for the north-light roofs of, for example, the Beyeler Foundation in Basel (1991–1997), the Nasher Sculpture Center in Dallas (1999–2003) and the Whitney Museum of American Art in New York (2003–2015).[31]

[1] For a detailed account of these years, see *Lorenzo Ciccarelli, Renzo Piano prima di Renzo Piano. I maestri e gli esordi*, Quodlibet/Renzo Piano Foundation, Macerata 2017.

[2] Ernst Jünger, *Al muro del tempo*, Adelphi, Milan 2000. The only exception is the Boschetto residential complex (1968–1970) built on the Erzilli Hill, which is well maintained and still lived in: see 'Un cantiere sperimentale. Case di Renzo Piano a Genova', in *Casabella*, 349, 1970, pp. 45–50.

[3] In 2015 an exhibition of several Building Workshop projects was held on the premises of the classical high school in Pegli that Piano had attended as a teenager: see *Renzo Piano Building Workshop. Progetti d'acqua*, Renzo Piano Foundation, Genoa 2015.

[4] Lorenzo Ciccarelli, op cit., 2017, pp. 21–45, 71–86. See also Daniela Bosia (ed.), *L'opera di Giuseppe Ciribini*, Franco Angeli, Milan 2013.

[5] Lorenzo Ciccarelli, op cit., 2017, pp. 49–58, 154–170. See also Marco Zanuso, Renzo Piano, Renato Lucci, *Elementi di tecnologia dei materiali come introduzione allo studio del design*, Tamburini, Milan 1967.

[6] See for example 'Italie 75', a monographic edition of *Architecture d'Aujourd'hui*, 181, 1975; 'Italian Architecture: 1945–1985', a monographic edition of a+u, 3, 1988; Jean-Louis Cohen, *La coupure entre architectes et intellectuels, ou les enseignements de l'italophilie*, École d'architecture de Paris-Villemin, Paris 1984; or the much more recent Denise Costanzo, Andrew Leach (eds.), *Italian Imprints on Twentieth-Century Architecture*, Bloomsbury, London 2022.

[7] Uliano Lucas, *Vivere a Ponente*, Vangelista, Milan 1989.

[8] Renzo Piano devoted the first edition of his *Giornale di bordo*, Passigli, Florence 1997, 'to my father who, for me as a child, was the greatest builder in the world'.

[9] In the dedication of the first edition of his *Giornale di bordo* (1997) Renzo Piano remembered Ermanno, who had died not long before, as 'the very best'.

[10] Renzo Piano, op cit., 1997, pp. 13–14. Nel 1992, a year after Ermanno's death, Piano established bursaries in memory of his 'builder brother', as a result of which a number of university students benefited from six-month internships in one of the RPBW studios.

[11] Renzo Piano Foundation, Projects Archive, Box 65P01. See also Massimo Dini, *Renzo Piano. Progetti e architetture* 1964–1983, Electa, Milan 1983, pp. 16–17.

[12] For Renzo Piano, the word *pezzo* (piece/component) has a programmatic value, denoting a form of architecture that is understated and rooted in constructional experimentation. Significantly, since 1982 almost all exhibitions of his work are entitled *Pezzo per pezzo*. See Gianpiero Donin (ed.), *Renzo Piano. Pezzo per pezzo*, Casa del libro, Rome 1982; 'Renzo Piano, Pezzo per pezzo', in Federico Bucci, Fulvio Irace (eds.), *Zero Gravity. Franco Albini, costruire le modernità*, Triennale Electa, Milan 2006, p. 189.

[13] The building was later altered, then demolished.

[14] Renzo Piano Foundation, Projects Archive, Box Pomezia 01. See also Renzo Piano, 'Ricerca sulle strutture in lamiera e in poliestere rinforzato', in *Domus*, 448, 1967, pp. 8–22; Massimo Dini 1983, op. cit., pp. 54–57.

[15] Renzo Piano still owns a first edition of Pier Luigi Nervi's celebrated handbook, *Costruire correttamente*, Hoepli, Milan 1955, copiously annotated.

[16] Tullia Iori, Sergio Poretti, 'Le opere di Pier Luigi Nervi alle Olimpiadi di Roma del 1960', in *Rassegna di Architettura e Urbanistica*, 121–122, 2007, pp. 105–119.

[17] See Claudio Greco, Pier Luigi Nervi. *Dai primi brevetti al Palazzo delle Esposizioni di Torino* 1917–1948, Quart, Lucerne 2008; Giulio Barazzetta (ed.), Pier Luigi Nervi. *Il modello come strumento di progetto e costruzione*, Quodlibet, Macerata 2017.

[18] Lorenzo Ciccarelli 2017, op. cit., pp. 89–96. Also: Renzo Piano, 'Entre la mémoire et l'oubli', in Raymond Guidot, Alain Guiheux (eds.), *Jean Prouvé 'constructeur'*, Éditions du Centre Pompidou, Paris, pp. 22–222.

[19] See Peter Sulzer, Jean Prouvé. *Oeuvre complète/Complete works*, 4 vols., Wasmuth-Birkhäuser, Tübingen-Basel 1995–2008.

[20] Françoise Chaslin, 'Il grande lattoniere Jean Prouvé', in Rassegna, 14, 1983, p. 55. See also Jean Prouvé. *The Poetics of Technical Object*, Skira, Geneva–Milan 2007.

[21] See Renzo Piano, *La responsabilità dell'architetto*, Passigli, Florence 2004, pp. 20–21.

[22] Giampiero Bosoni, 'La via italiana alle materie plastiche', in Rassegna, 14, 1983, pp. 42–53; Alessandra Rinaldi, *Evoluzione delle materie plastiche nel design per l'edilizia* 1945–1990, Franco Angeli, Milan 2014.

[23] It was no coincidence that the first studio that Renzo Piano organized in Milan a few months after graduating, with his course mates Renato Foni, Gianni Garbuglia, Lino Tirelli and Maurizio Filocco, was called Studio Ricerca e Progettazione (Research and Planning Studio).

[24] Flavio Marano, 'La calcolatrice con la radice quadrata', in *Abitare*, 497, 2009, p. 132. In addition: the author's conversation with Flavio Marano, Genoa, 25 May 2021.

[25] Renzo Piano Foundation, Projects Archive, Boxes 69OFF01 and 68ST01.

[26] Renzo Piano 1967, op. cit.

[27] Winfried Nerdinger (ed.), Frei Otto. *Complete Works. Lightweight Construction, Natural Design*, Birkhäuser, Basel-Boston 2005. See also the monographic number of *Architectural Design*, Frei Otto at Work, 3, 1971, owned and heavily annotated by Piano.

[28] Lorenzo Ciccarelli 2017, op. cit., pp. 238–248.

[29] See Edgar Stach, *Renzo Piano Building Workshop. Space-Detail-Light*, Birkhäuser, Basel 2021.

[30] Renzo Piano, 'Uno studio-laboratorio', in *Domus*, 479, 1969, pp. 10–14.

[31] Following the examples of Nervi and Prouvé, in these early years Piano patented the most interesting construction systems and components with which he was experimenting. This was the case, for example, with this north-light roofing panel in reinforced polyester. See Lorenzo Ciccarelli 2017, op. cit., pp. 122–127.

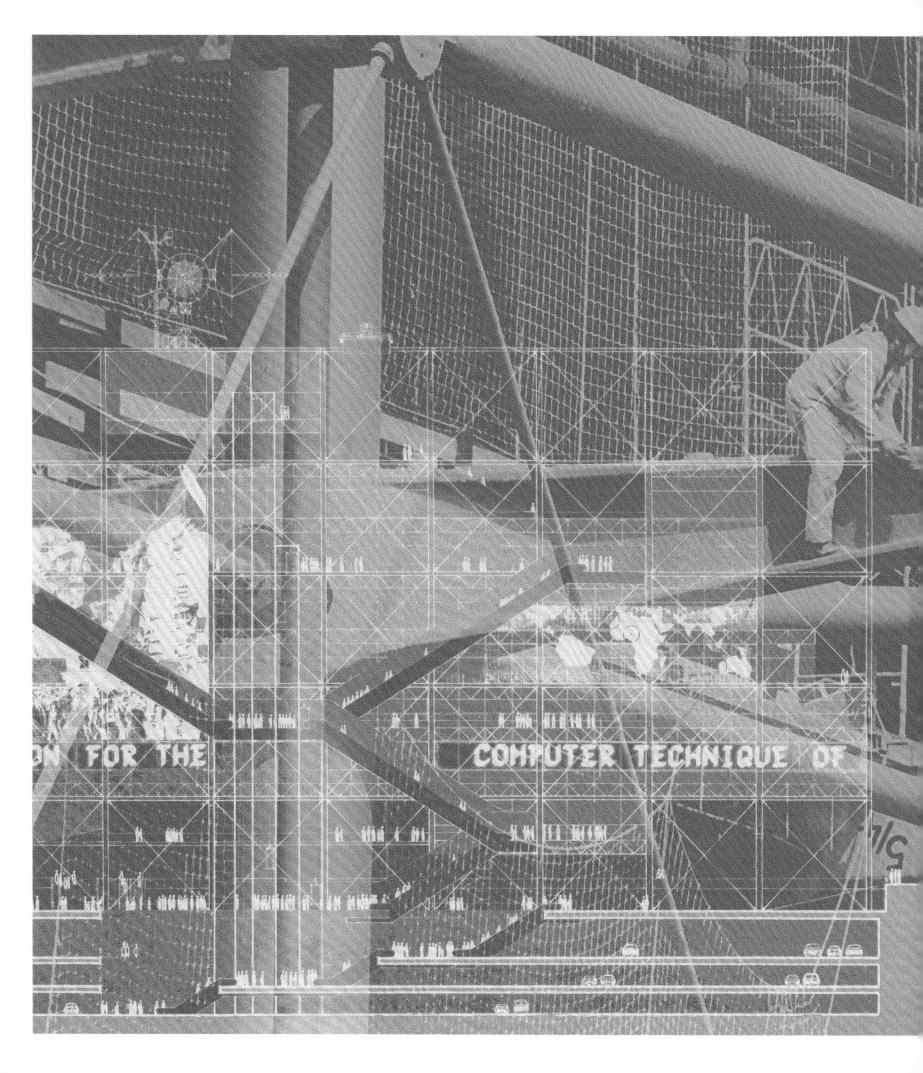

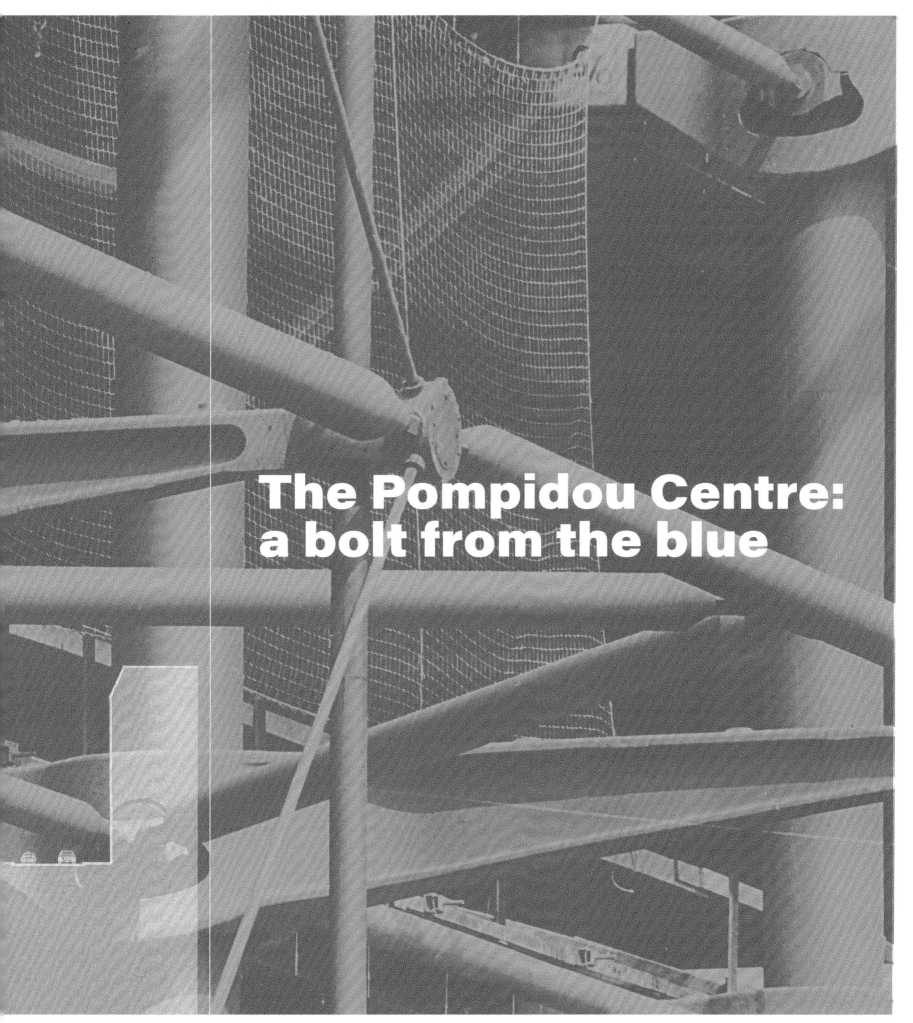

The Pompidou Centre: a bolt from the blue

In the almost endless sequence of images recording the sensational success of the Georges Pompidou Centre (1971–1977) in the Beaubourg district of Paris, there is one that, more than all the others, reveals the deeper meaning of this great venture. It is a photomontage of many of the people who for seven years contributed to the planning and construction of the celebrated building. They are not posed in the conventional way, one beside the other around Renzo Piano and Richard Rogers, but revolve riotously around them, some upside down, some on top of one another, some appearing more than once.[1]

This was what Beaubourg was like for those closely involved: a bolt from the blue that revolutionized the small-scale, bread-and-butter work that Renzo Piano and Richard and Su Rogers were doing in Genoa and London. For these young architects, hitherto virtually unknown, it was the entrance into a political, social and media circus. They were catapulted into a collective undertaking dictated by a mad rush to deliver drawings – some 25,000 were required, controversies and legal disputes, and a building project of extraordinary complexity bang in the historic heart of Paris.[2]

While in painting and sculpture the hand of a single artist may be sufficient, architecture is a collective endeavour that demands the conjunction of diverse and complementary people and skills. A building combines and expresses the stories of a multitude of players who, over the duration of a project, determine its many twists and turns: the clients, the public authorities, the architects, engineers, technicians, designers and fitters, the suppliers and worksite managers, the building contractors and so on – a collective dimension of encounters and friendships forged during the development of a project which continue to have echoes down the years.

COLLAGE PUT TOGETHER BY
SUNJI ISHIDA FOR RICHARD
ROGERS' BIRTHDAY IN 1974,
FEATURING SOME OF THE PIANO
& ROGERS ARCHITECTS AND
ENGINEERS WHO WORKED
ON THE POMPIDOU CENTRE.

needs of the new millennium (1997–2000).[5] And for more than fifty years the Paris headquarters of the Building Workshop have been housed just a few hundred metres from Beaubourg, initially in the Rue Sainte-Croix de la Bretonnerie, then in the Rue des Archives. The architects who work in the present building need only walk round the corner to glimpse the colourful ducting on the side of the building on the Rue du Renard.

But we need to step back a bit to explain the characteristics of an operation which remains one of the most extraordinary of the 20th century.

On 5 June 1969, Georges Pompidou (1911–1974) succeeded General Charles de Gaulle as President of France. To re-energize the Fifth Republic – overshadowed politically and culturally by the United States in the new world order that emerged from World War II and weakened by the tumultuous

AERIAL PHOTOGRAPH OF THE MARAIS DISTRICT WITH THE BEAUBOURG PLATEAU AREA WHERE THE CULTURAL CENTRE WAS TO BE BUILT COLOURED IN ORANGE. IN THE CENTRE-RIGHT ARE THE PAVILIONS OF LES HALLES, THE HISTORIC COVERED MARKET DESIGNED BY VICTOR BALTARD, WHICH WAS SUBSEQUENTLY DEMOLISHED.

Beaubourg was more than a straightforward construction project for Renzo Piano.[3] During its long gestation, he got to know and recruited some of his key colleagues in what was to become the Building Workshop – Bernard Plattner, Shunji Ishida and Noriaki Okabe, as well as working with engineers Peter Rice (1935–1992) and Tom Barker (1937–2021) from the Ove Arup & Partners practice, who, as we shall see, became outstanding consultants and supporters in his most significant projects in the period up to the mid-1990s.[4]

The link between Piano and Beaubourg has never been broken. Even after the inauguration of the cultural centre on 31 January 1977, he continued to work on the great 'spaceship', adding new bits, such as the Ircam musical research centre (1973–1990) and the Atelier Brancusi exhibition area (1991–1996), or getting it fit and ready for the

THE FRONT ELEVATION OF THE PLAN FOR THE 1971 COMPETITION FOR A "REAL-TIME INFORMATION CENTRE" CHARACTERIZED BY FLEXIBILITY, OPENNESS AND COMBINATION OF KNOW-HOW.

protest movement of May 1968 – Pompidou wanted to promote the creation of a great centre featuring contemporary art and culture. What was initially intended to be 'simply' a national contemporary art centre was gradually invested with new functions to the point of becoming a multidisciplinary building for experimentation and the dissemination of contemporary culture.[6] The President set up a structure independent of the Ministry of Culture and the municipal authorities to direct and supervise the entire administrative process, as well as the planning and actual construction of the cultural centre. It included experienced civil servants such as Sébastien Loste and François Lombard, and oversight of the project was entrusted to Robert Bordaz (1908–1996), who played a vital part in the success of the operation, as Piano never failed to acknowledge.[7]

With the political end in view, the announcement of the competition – published in November 1970 and, exceptionally, open to architects from all over the world, without reservation as to nationality, age, experience or financial capacity – called for a complex of roughly 96,000 square metres that would house 'a reception area; a public library; a modern and contemporary art museum; a design museum; an industrial production centre; multipurpose rooms for drama, music and film shows; temporary exhibition rooms; and facilities for specialized research and documentation'. It was to be erected on the Beaubourg plateau – an area then used as a car park in the historic Marais district, and not far from Les Halles, the old covered market designed by Victor Baltard.[8]

In January 1971, the structural engineer Ted Happold, head of the Structure 3 Division of Ove

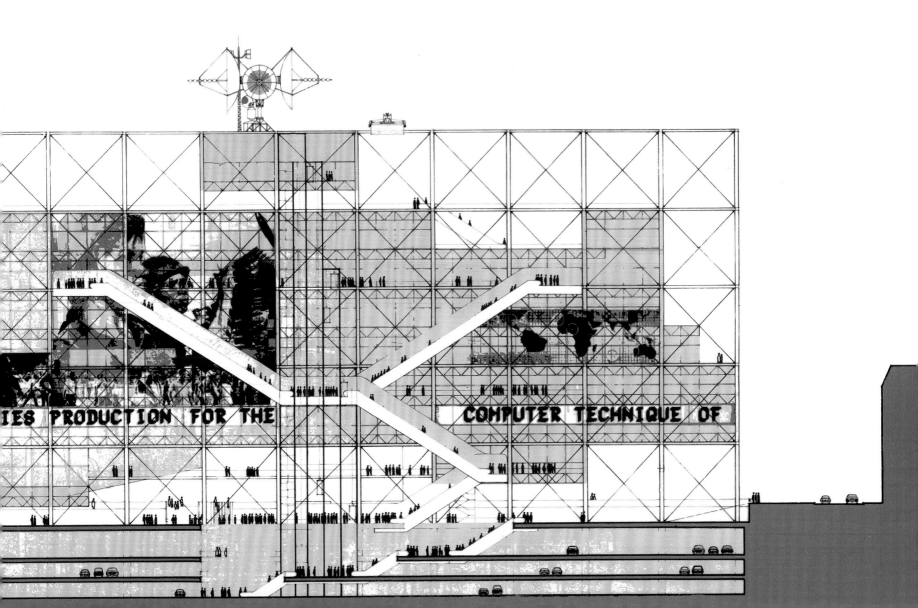

IES PRODUCTION FOR THE   COMPUTER TECHNIQUE OF

Arup & Partners, which also included Lennart Grut and Peter Rice, learned of the competition and decided to participate.[9] He saw it as a golden opportunity to apply on a large scale the research on steel structures made of cast components that Structure 3 had been working on for several years, following the example of the German engineer Frei Otto.[10]

A similar approach had been adopted for the retractable roof of Chelsea Football Stadium in London, designed a few months earlier by Structure 3 in conjunction with a couple of young English architects, Richard and Su Rogers, who meanwhile had got to know an Italian colleague recently moved to London with whom they were to set up shop in those early months of 1971: Renzo Piano.[11]

Given that only architects were allowed to participate in the Beaubourg competition, Happold, on behalf of Ove Arup & Partners, asked Richard and Su Rogers to come on board with them, also offering to pay the entry fee.

After several years in the United States, and the experience of Team 4 with Norman and Wendy Foster, in 1967 Richard and Su Rogers had struck out on their own, working on a series of experimental projects featuring prefabricated building shells that could be modified and were characterized by open and flexible interiors, made of lightweight materials not generally used in the construction industry.

For example, their Zip-Up Houses (1967–1969) were residential modules erected on steel columns that offered maximum internal flexibility and could be adapted to all types of terrain and infinitely expanded by adding further wall panels in series.[12]

Their meeting with Renzo Piano – who had first visited London in 1964 to share his research findings with the Anglo-Polish engineer Zygmunt Makowski, and then had moved there more or less permanently in 1969 – therefore occurred quite naturally. Piano and Rogers shared a similar approach to projects and had done similar research: prefabricated building techniques; stringent integration of structure and services; the creation of flexible space; and experimentation with plastic materials in architecture.

So this is how the following diverse group of people came together to draw up the competition proposal and, once they had been awarded the contract, plan and build Beaubourg: Ove Arup & Partners (more specifically Structure 3) together with Piano and Richard and Su Rogers, who called on friends and colleagues to contribute, in particular John Young, Marco Goldschmied and Gianfranco Franchini.[13] Piano & Rogers' research on flexible space and prefabricated structures, together with Structure 3's interest in metal frameworks using cast components, were key aspects of the competition entry.[14] A decisive factor was the decision to apply in a project of vastly greater

WORK ON THE STRUCTURE OF THE BUILDING BEGAN IN OCTOBER 1974 AND WAS COMPLETED IN ROUGHLY NINE MONTHS. EACH BAY TOOK TEN DAYS TO ERECT.

size and complexity the same design method the two architects had experimented with in their small-scale buildings. The principles of spatial flexibility and adaptability, ensured by a lightweight prefabricated load-bearing structure, were instrumental in enabling them to adhere as faithfully as possible to the requirements of the specification.

Piano & Rogers condensed the many and diverse functions required by the programme into a five-floor rectangular volume, 170 metres long and 50 metres wide – a 'live information centre' characterized by a series of uncluttered horizontal surfaces that could be subdivided using mobile partitions to meet the needs of the moment.[15]

The imperative of internal flexibility meant that the structural components and ducting for the various services had to be pushed out to the perimeter, located within an open space frame around the building, also serving as a support structure for the escalators and for screens and other audio-visual apparatus.[16]

LEFT TO RIGHT:
RICHARD ROGERS,
MARCO GOLDSCHMIED,
SU ROGERS, JOHN YOUNG
AND RENZO PIANO.

BELOW: THE *GERBERETTES*,
ENORMOUS STEEL CANTILEVERS,
FRESHLY CAST IN THE
GERMAN FOUNDRY.

While the British experience of Richard and Su Rogers – and the influence of so revolutionary a project as Cedric Price's Fun Palace (1959–1961) – were very influential in defining the aesthetics of the building itself, it was the Italian cultural and urban roots of Piano and Rogers that inspired the *parvis*: the wide open space which, like the square in front of a church, exposes the living mass of the building to the air of the city. It is no coincidence that in the drawings for the competition entry it is indicated, in Italian, by the word *piazza*. This decision was also motivated by the fact that the cultural centre had to fit into the Marais, the most densely populated district of Paris, which also lacked a public space. The decision not to occupy the whole of the designated site, but to have the building back onto the Rue du Renard, thus turning half of the Beaubourg Plateau into a public square, was a decisive factor in determining the jury's choice of the Piano & Rogers project.[17] The *parvis* was not a requirement of the competition specification, and in almost all the other proposals the building occupied the entire site.[18]

On 5 July 1971, the international jury – chaired by Jean Prouvé and consisting of Gaëtan Picon, Frank Francis, Michel Laclotte, Herman Liebaers, Willem Sandberg, Émile Aillaud, Philip Johnson, Oscar Niemeyer and Robert Regard – began examining the 682 entries submitted to them. After a rigorous, multi-stage process of shortlisting and discussion, the members of the jury pronounced their verdict, by eight votes out of nine, in favour of project number 493. Jean Prouvé recorded that 'when the sealed envelope was opened, and the name of Piano & Rogers was read out, there was silence. No one had the slightest idea who they were.'[19]

When Piano and Rogers received the news of their victory, they could rely on the support of only a restricted number of employees, with no experience of major projects. Beaubourg was not built by an organized professional practice with a clearly defined hierarchy forged in the white heat of other major projects, but by a group of young Italian, British, American, Swiss, Austrian, Dutch, Greek and Japanese architects starting out on their careers.[20]

The enormous difficulties that arose between the award of the contract and the signing-off of the project are well known: the death in 1974 of Georges Pompidou, the principal champion of the Centre; the suspicion and mistrust with which some of the clients, public opinion and the French business system regarded the two young architects; and the increasing misunderstandings with Ove Arup & Partners, who seemed to think that Piano & Rogers were not capable of completing the construction of Beaubourg.[21]

Under obligation to submit an *Avant-Projet Sommaire* (short preliminary plan) within a few months of winning the competition, the mixed group of architects brought together by Piano and Rogers grew and changed many times; not until 1972/73 did a stable form

THE REAR ELEVATION OF THE BUILDING ON THE RUE DU RENARD AND, OPPOSITE, THE TWO VAST OPEN SQUARES – THE PLACE GEORGES POMPIDOU AND THE PLACE IGOR STRAVINSKY – THAT FLANK THE CULTURAL CENTRE IN THE DENSELY POPULATED MARAIS DISTRICT.

THE 'JOYOUS MACHINE' OF THE
POMPIDOU CENTRE RISES ABOVE
THE ROOFS OF THE MARAIS
DISTRICT. AT FIRST BITTERLY
CONTESTED, TODAY IT IS ONE OF
THE MOST ADMIRED SYMBOLS
OF PARIS.

'Our utopian vision was that the Pompidou Centre should not be a building but a tool. That was the great challenge of Beaubourg and it still is. I continue to hope that increasingly it will become something that is used, and so will avoid the danger of becoming a monument.' Renzo Piano

of organization emerge. They were joined in Paris by, among others, Mike Davies, Alan Stanton, Laurie Abbott, Shunji Ishida – a Japanese architect who had worked with Ove Arup & Partners – Noriaki Okabe, Hiroshi Naruse, Yuki Takahashi, Cuno Brullman, Walter Zbinden, Reyner Verbizh and Bernard Plattner, the latter with the task of liaising between the architects and the contractors on site.[22]

While the project was gradually being defined, Piano and Rogers had to abandon some of the points that had featured in the competition entry, for example having movable floors or using the space frame of the facade as an audio-visual medium, while confirming others: from the prefabricated metal structure with cast joints to the continuity between the *parvis* and the ground floor of the building.[23]

THE ENTRANCE TO THE
POMPIDOU CENTRE AS
ORIGINALLY CONFIGURED.

The town planning regulation that limited the maximum height of the building to 42 metres led to one of the most amazing aspects of the project as eventually realized. The Piazza del Campo in Siena, on a slope and shell-shaped, admired by both Rogers and Piano, and referred to by the latter in some of his articles in the 1960s, was inspirational in their design of the sloping open space of the Beaubourg plateau. This means that visitors literally gravitate to the entrance of the building, which is located below street level.[24]

Having defined the spatial layout, the designers turned their attention to the most problematic aspects of the project: defining the structural cage and planning the services.

The decision to place the ducting for the services and the visitor traffic systems – the lifts and the famous escalators that distinguish the elevation facing the parvis – on the perimeter of the open floor areas transformed the shell of Beaubourg into a three-dimensional space frame. This meant extending the paired Warren trusses that spanned the width of the building by a further 5 metres – making them 45 metres in length and 2.5 metres in height – and designing a component to connect the heads of the trusses with the light structural steel framework of the elevations. This component was the famous *gerberette*, long studied by Lennart Grut and Peter Rice: the *pezzo* shaped and cast in the Krupp steelworks in Germany, which also supplied other components for assembling the structural skeleton of the building.[25]

Every *gerberette* – named after Heinrich Gerber (1832–1912), the German engineer who first

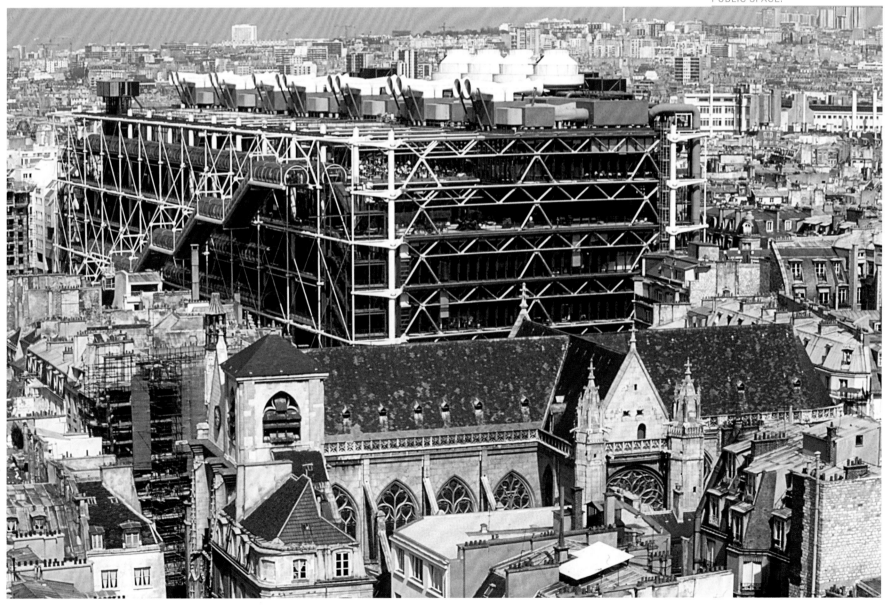

THE *PARVIS*, THE SLOPING OPEN SPACE IN FRONT OF THE POMPIDOU CENTRE, SOON BECAME ONE OF THE LIVELIEST PARTS OF THE MARAIS DISTRICT.

theorized and employed similar cantilevers in the iron bridges he designed in the late 19th and early 20th centuries – is 8.2 metres long and weighs 9.6 tonnes. Following many refinements and trials in the foundry, it was possible to produce each *gerberette* in a single casting, the surest way of avoiding weaknesses and areas of fragility.[26] The *gerberettes* are the best expression of what Peter Rice wanted from the structural components: he believed that they should show evidence of 'human handiwork' – in other words, the intellectual labour and craftsmanship with which industrial materials should be processed – to mediate between the humanity of the visitor and the impersonality of the building.[27] This was a structural approach and a working method to which Piano could not but subscribe.

The designers decided to accommodate the ducting carrying the services in the cavity between the two metal frameworks that defined the outward shape of the building. The planning for this was managed by Tom Barker (1937–2021), an Ove Arup & Partners engineer, assisted by the Piano & Rogers architects, in particular Shunji Ishida.[28] The tubes carrying the various services were grouped together on the basis of their diameters and painted in bright colours according to their functions – plumbing, electrical, ventilation, etc. Running untrammelled over the elevations of the building, they added an aesthetic dimension, as well as fulfilling their essentially functional role.[29] In this way Piano and Rogers assimilated the lesson that Reyner Banham had tried to impart in *The Architecture of the Well-Tempered Environment* (1969), which, according to Shunji Ishida, 'was one of the few books constantly on our drawing board while we were planning Beaubourg': technological research, far from being a prescriptive science restricted to engineers, can and must become the instrument whereby the architect interprets, rather than suffers, modernity.[30]

Construction work on Beaubourg began on 23 May 1972. The first bay was erected on 31 October 1974, and in April 1975 the structural cage was completed. However, the Piano & Rogers architects continued to work on the building well beyond the date of its inauguration, which took place on 31 January 1977 in the presence of the French President Valéry Giscard d'Estaing.

As stated at the beginning, Piano never really severed his connection with Beaubourg. In 2018, for an exhibition of his works at the Royal Academy of Arts in London, he ordered a life-size model of a *gerberette*, boldly painted red. When the exhibition ended, Piano decided to transport it to Genoa to grace the entrance to the Building Workshop, and dedicated it to the memory of Peter Rice.

[1] The collage, created by Shunji Ishida in 1974 for Richard Rogers' birthday, is published in Lia Piano (ed.), *Piano+Rogers. Centre Pompidou*, Renzo Piano Foundation, Genoa 2017, p. 45.

[2] No end of books and articles have been written about the Pompidou Centre. I would mention only the writings of Nathan Silver, *The Making of Beaubourg*, MIT Press, Cambridge (MA) 1994 and Francesco Dal Co, *Centre Pompidou. Renzo Piano, Richard Rogers and the Making of a Modern Monument*, Yale Press, New Haven 2017. More recently, the doctoral thesis of Boris Hamzeian, Centre National d'Art et de Culture Georges Pompidou. Cronache di idea, progetto e fabbricazione, 1968–1977 (École Polytechnique Fédérale de Lausanne, 2021) has provided a substantial amount of new information and archive material.

[3] See the conversation between Renzo Piano and Richard Rogers in Lia Piano (ed.) 2017, op. cit., pp. 189–210.

[4] Shunji Ishida, 'Direi che la cosa funziona', in *Being Renzo Piano*, monographic edition of *Abitare*, 497, 2009, pp. 133–134; Bernard Plattner, 'Il ruolo dello svizzero', in the same publication, pp. 152–153.

[5] Renzo Piano, *Giornale di bordo*, Passigli, Florence 2005, pp. 152–153, 212–215, 292–299.

[6] Boris Hamzeian 2021, in op. cit., gives a detailed account of the various political and institutional steps, beginning in the early 1960s, that led to the definition of a new Centre National d'Art Contemporain, culminating in the Beaubourg project.

[7] See Robert Bordaz, *Renzo Piano, Entretiens*, Éditions Cercle D'Art, Paris 1997.

[8] Renzo Piano, Richard Rogers, *Du Plateau Beaubourg au Centre Georges Pompidou*, Éditions du Centre Georges Pompidou, Paris 1987, p. 52.

[9] Boris Hamzeian 2021, op. cit., pp. 105, 128ff.

[10] Francesco Dal Co 2017, op. cit., pp. 15–21.

[11] Lorenzo Ciccarelli, *Renzo Piano prima di Renzo Piano. I maestri e gli esordi*, Quodlibet/Renzo Piano Foundation, Macerata 2017, pp. 207–228.

[12] See Dejan Sudjic, *The Architecture of Richard Rogers*, Fourth Estate and Wordsearch, London 1994, pp. 11–51; Kenneth Powell, *Richard Rogers. Complete Works, Vol. I*, Phaidon, London 1999, pp. 8–57.

[13] Nathan Silver 1994, op. cit., pp. 13–17, 62–66.

[14] Boris Hamzeian 2021, op. cit., p. 141.

[15] Ted Happold, Peter Rice, 'Centre Beaubourg: Introduction', in *The Arup Journal*, 2, 1973, p. 3.

[16] The competition proposal is published in Lia Piano (ed.) 2017, op. cit., pp. 12–17.

[17] Boris Hamzeian 2021, op. cit., pp. 181–182.

[18] Susan Holden, 'Possible Pompidous', in *AA Files*, 70, 2015, pp. 33–59.

[19] Nathan Silver 1994, op. cit., p. 41.

[20] From 1972, Piano, Rogers and many of their colleagues moved to Paris, while the Ove Arup & Partners engineers mostly remained in London.

[21] Boris Hamzeian 2021, op. cit., pp. 317ff.

[22] Conversation between the author and Bernard Plattner, Paris, 30 November 2018.

[23] Ted Happold, Peter Rice 1973, op. cit., p. 3. Some of the project drawings produced in these years are kept at the Renzo Piano Foundation, Projects Archive, Piano & Rogers Collection, Centre Georges Pompidou 1970–1977.

[24] Renzo Piano, 'Renzo Piano', in *Architectural Design*, 3, 1970, pp. 140–145. See also Enrique Walker, 'Renzo Piano & Richard Rogers in conversation with Enrique Walker', in *AA Files*, 70, 2015, p. 50.

[25] Peter Rice, *An Engineer Imagines*, Ellipsis, London 1994, pp. 32–33.

[26] Ivi, pp. 37–40.

[27] Ivi, p. 77.

[28] Conversation between the author and Shunji Ishida, Genoa, 30 July 2020.

[29] Boris Hamzeian 2021, op. cit., pp. 198–207, 545–549.

[30] Reyner Banham, *The Architecture of the Well-Tempered Environment*, Architectural Press, London 1969. For the quotation: conversation between the author and Shunji Ishida, Genoa, 1 September 2015.

The wilderness years

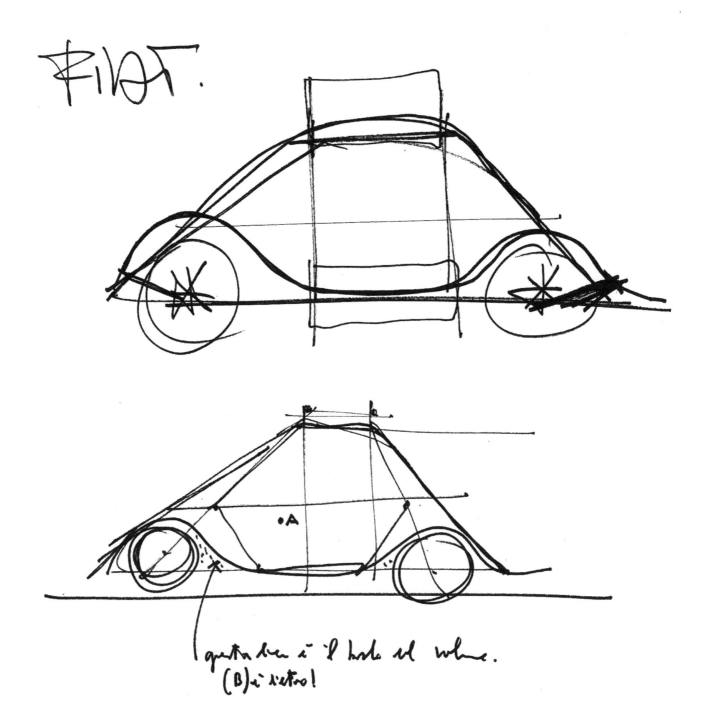

FIAT.

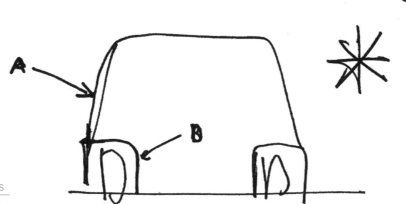

The opening of the Pompidou Centre on 31 January 1977 and the public acclaim that greeted the new building were no guarantee of immediate and commensurate professional success for Renzo Piano. The innovative impact of Beaubourg – a unique, unclassifiable 'artefact', a hybrid phenomenon combining craftsmanship and an industrial aesthetic, a futuristic engineered structure and an open, flexible space – was not fully acceptable in the Italian architectural culture of the time.[1]

Having ended his partnership with Richard Rogers, who the following year was commissioned to design an important new headquarters for Lloyd's of London, Piano returned to Italy, to Genoa, where for several years he concentrated on a series of minor projects marked by his collaboration with Peter Rice and performed by a much-reduced number of colleagues. The four years between the inauguration of the Pompidou Centre and the commission for the Menil Collection could be described as Piano's wilderness years. Living a provincial life far from the bright lights of Paris, working more as a DIY enthusiast than as a conventional architect, he engaged in projects involving experimentation with materials and techniques, applying them to a series of creations involving product design and planning for prefabricated buildings, and to strategies for non-invasive interventions in historic town centres.[2]

In Genoa, in the garden of his house in Pegli, Piano built a glazed conservatory to serve as his studio, which he shared with just a few colleagues: Flavio Marano, Shunji Ishida, Noriaki Okabe, Giorgio Fascioli, Ottavio Di Blasi, Enrico Frigerio, Renzo Venanzio Truffelli, François Doria and the model-maker Rinaldo Gaggero, a former naval carpenter.[3] Nevertheless, Piano decided to maintain a working office in Paris, mainly to complete the executive and internal planning of Beaubourg, and then to look for further work in France. Based there at 14 Rue Sainte-Croix de la Bretonnerie were Bernard Plattner, Walter Zbinden, Reiner Verbizh, Mike Dowd and Johanna Lohse.[4]

In 1977 Piano changed the name of his practice to Atelier Piano & Rice.

The collaboration between Renzo Piano and Peter Rice should not be seen as a permanent professional partnership: Rice was Piano's most favoured colleague on many of the projects he undertook during those years, but not on every occasion.[5] They were both driven by curiosity and a burning desire to experiment, and the elective affinity sparked off by the Beaubourg project was fuelled by a mutual methodological instinct to combine and blend their different areas of competence.[6] The projects on which they worked together demonstrate their curiosity and desire to apply the methods of industrial production to architecture, as well as the conviction that the industrialization of architecture should not eliminate the contribution made by human ingenuity and the craftsman's love of creating a *pezzo*, but should exhibit the 'humanistic' matrix of engineering design.[7] This multidisciplinary tension was reflected in the choice of projects and activities taken on by Atelier Piano & Rice: an experimental vehicle for Fiat (1978–1979) designed to considerably reduce the weight of the car body; a series of documentaries on the history of architecture for the RAI (Italian broadcasting corporation) (1979); the construction of a housing complex using prefabricated components at Corciano (1978–1982); or the Laboratori di Quartiere (District Workshops) experiment (1979–1980). These experimental projects went beyond architecture as conventionally understood but enabled the two designers to formulate innovative solutions and explore the characteristics of materials and industrial processes that Piano was later to redeploy.

► In 1978 Nicola Tufarelli, managing director of Fiat, commissioned Piano and Rice to design a prototype motor vehicle that would give fresh impetus to the company: an innovative automobile designed to take advantage of new materials and the most advanced production and assembly techniques, with a target of reducing the weight of the vehicle by at least 20 per cent.[8]

Why entrust such a task to an architect and a structural engineer, both lacking previous experience of automobile design, rather than to one of the many qualified motor vehicle engineers on whose services Fiat could rely?

The decision was probably motivated by the conviction that, to achieve real innovation, it was necessary to draw on people from outside the industry who were not hampered by the technical conditioning and production constraints to which all cars were subject. Besides, in constructing the Pompidou Centre, Piano and Rice had shown that they designed buildings like 'machines': painstakingly studying the materials on which the design of mass-produced components was based and assembling them to make the final product.

To develop the VSS – Vettura Sperimentale a Sottosistemi (experimental vehicle and subsystems) – a research centre, the I.De.A. (Institute of Development in Automotive Engineering), was set up, administered by car designer Franco Mantegazza and directed by Piano, with Rice as vice-president. The Institute was housed in an 18th-century villa in the Moncalieri Hills, located fairly close but still at a significant distance

THE PRIMARY STRUCTURE PIANO AND RICE DESIGNED FOR THE VSS WAS CHARACTERIZED BY HIGH MECHANICAL PERFORMANCE AND WAS EXTREMELY LIGHT WEIGHT.

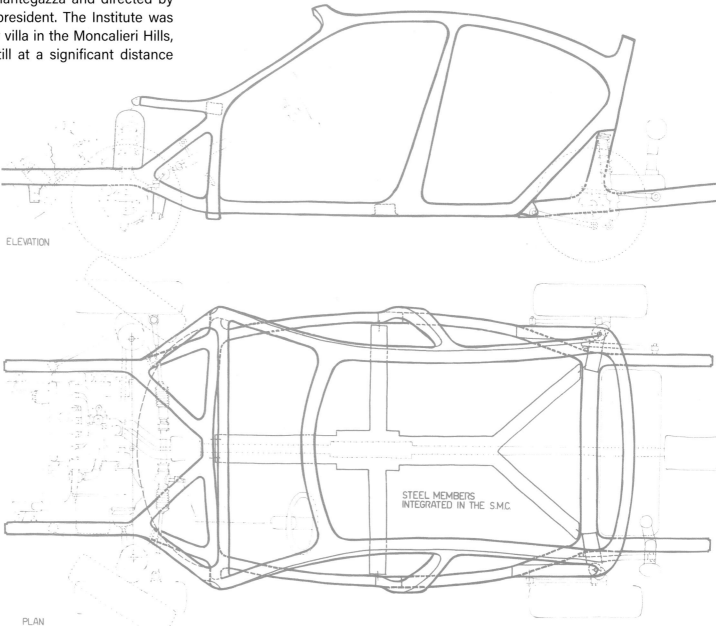

ELEVATION

STEEL MEMBERS INTEGRATED IN THE S.M.C.

PLAN

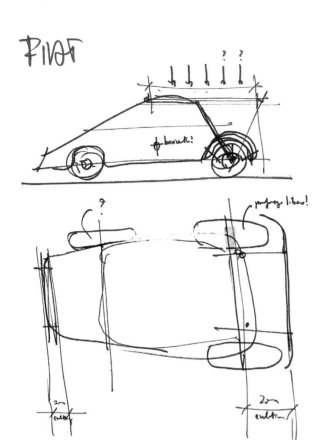

from the Fiat headquarters in Lingotto, to make the point that this was a separate venture, albeit undertaken in synergy with the parent company.

Piano and Rice tackled the project by first taking apart a traditional motor vehicle and studying its components, concluding that to renovate the production process and significantly reduce the weight of the vehicle it was necessary to separate the structural framework from the body.[9] In developing the VSS, Piano applied the same principles – prefabrication of components and use of plastic materials – as for his experimental structures of the 1960s, believing that the technology of the automobile industry could be viewed in terms of architecture and vice versa. They designed the VSS with the same criteria as a building, making a conceptual and constructional separation between the load-bearing structure and the lightweight infill parts.

By shifting the structural, strength-imparting functions to the chassis, carefully studied and designed by Rice, it was possible to do away with the heavy sheet-metal car body, as conceived up to that time, and develop a significantly lighter body of plastic material. They experimented with polypropylene, polyurethane, polyester, polycarbonates and nylon to obtain individual parts – door components, bonnet components, roof components, etc. – that could be modelled in various shapes, and assembled and dismantled, thus achieving different motor vehicle configurations on the same chassis.[10] The separation of chassis and body also ensured improved acoustic performance, vibrations from the body being absorbed by joints made from elastic material. Finally, this approach made it possible to revolutionize the production process, dissociating the production of the chassis from the making of the body components, which could be outsourced in the same way as the minor items of equipment, all culminating in the final act of assembling the finished motor vehicle.

Between 1978 and 1979, Piano and Rice carefully studied the shape and structure of the VSS using models and the wind tunnel, working closely with Fiat's engineers and consultants. Although the prototype was not produced and put into production when their involvement with Fiat came to an end, ten years later, in 1988, the company launched the Tipo, which embodied many of the concepts first developed for the VSS.

RENZO PIANO AND PETER RICE WORKED CLOSELY TOGETHER, SO MUCH SO THAT IT WAS IMPOSSIBLE TO DISTINGUISH THE INPUTS OF THE ARCHITECT FROM THOSE OF THE ENGINEER.

▶ While engaged in designing the prototype of the VSS, Piano agreed to devise and produce a television programme for RAI. *Cantiere aperto* (Open worksite), as it was interestingly entitled, was a series of ten episodes – edited by Piano with the screenplay written by his wife and sharp-minded colleague Magda Arduino – broadcast by RAI in 1979 as part of *Habitat*, a well-received programme anchored by Giulio Macchi (1918–2009), the first person in Italy to present ideas about the built environment to the public.[11] The short sequences devised by Piano and his colleagues were intended to 're-establish the relationship between consumer and builder'[12] – a series of visual lessons that sought to 'demystify construction techniques for non-specialists and make them comprehensible and accessible'. They tackled the worksites of the medieval cathedrals, ingenious uses of materials such as timber and steel, ways of creating more space by digging underground or using the roof void and, finally, the idea of evolutive space. Explanations of the fundamentals of building, the development of materials, their processing and use in combination were continually illustrated by models or prototypes constructed live on TV by associated architects Shunji Ishida and Noriaki Okabe and colleagues Sugako Yamada and Manuela Bonino.[13]

'We need to recombine the different skills,' stated Piano, 'and rediscover an idea of architecture that has been lost for centuries; architecture as planning, building, the invention of production processes and even tools, not limited merely to making things that look nice.' In this sense, the medieval cathedral worksite provided a meaningful model, regarded as 'a place where no distinction was made between intellectual and manual activities', where sense of space and ingenuity of construction met, and the master builder might well be called on to invent tools and machines for moving materials.[14] The principle of co-construction as the fruit of scientific research and experimentation with models was constantly emphasized during the TV broadcasts. It was demonstrated, for example, by the construction of an innovative roof truss in which every stressed wooden component was replaced

LEFT TO RIGHT: SUGAKO YAMADA, MANUELA BONINO AND RENZO PIANO STANDING AROUND THE MODEL OF A YURT FOR THE *CANTIERE APERTO* TV BROADCAST, IN 1979.

by slim steel cables, or emergency shelters consisting of sheets of plywood stiffened as required by putting them under tension. In exhibiting these prototypes, Piano wanted to show how 'research in the construction field does not necessarily mean complex instrumentation or sophisticated systems,' while the anti-conventional use of cheap or recycled materials could lead to the building of innovative structures for immediate use.

The tents of desert-dwelling Tuaregs or the yurts of Mongol people were good examples of this approach. 'A Tuareg's dwelling is a tool,' insisted Piano, 'an instrument for the nomadic lifestyle.' In the same way, the yurt was interpreted as a house/tool made of standardized components. These dwellings were light and easy to transport, to erect and to modify, to meet the changing needs of their occupants; they were lean structures involving nothing superfluous. While they were reconstructing the model of the yurt or demonstrating the rapid balloon-frame construction system using planks of

MOCK-UP OF THE DIFFERENT EPISODES, AND HOW THEY WOULD BE PRESENTED, IN PREPARATION FOR THE *CANTIERE APERTO* BROADCASTS.

wood and nails adopted by the American pioneers – both prefabricated and easy to transport on carts or waggons, Piano insisted on 'the quality of lightweight construction techniques, which for us is synonymous with strict and sparing use of materials, ease of assembly and thrift on the part of the consumer'.

All these ideas were drawn together in the final episode of *Cantiere aperto*, which was devoted to evolutive living: the idea of free and flexible living space. This was a concept with which Piano was experimenting in his Evolutive Housing project (1978), part of the reconstruction campaign following a serious earthquake in Friuli Venezia Giulia, and applied extensively in the Il Rigo residential neighbourhood of Corciano (1978–1982).[15]

▶ For his Evolutive Housing prototype, Piano defined both a primary and a secondary structure: the former being the business of the architect, the latter the concern of the future occupant of the housing unit. The role of the architect was to design the load-bearing structure of the building and its external walls, while the occupant was entrusted with the task of subdividing the internal space. The aim of this strategy to involve the future occupants in the process of defining the building was inspired by the 'participatory' planning that Giancarlo De Carlo (1919–2005) had tried to apply in his work on the working-class Matteotti district of Terni (1969–1975).[16]

The Evolutive Housing prototype, designed by Piano and Rice and developed with Vibrocemento of Perugia (now Generale Prefabbricati), was entered for the 1976 competition for post-earthquake reconstruction in Friuli Venezia Giulia.[17] The module consisted of an earthquake-proof structure of channel sections in reinforced concrete assembled into a monolithic 6 x 6 metre box forming the floor, side walls and ceiling of the housing unit. The two open walls were infilled

THE FACT THAT THE APARTMENTS WERE MODULAR AND COULD BE MODIFIED IN LAYOUT AND NUMBER OF FLOORS WAS THE KEY FEATURE OF BOTH THE EVOLUTIVE HOUSING PROTOTYPE AND THE IL RIGO NEIGHBOURHOOD OF CORCIANO, 1978–1982.

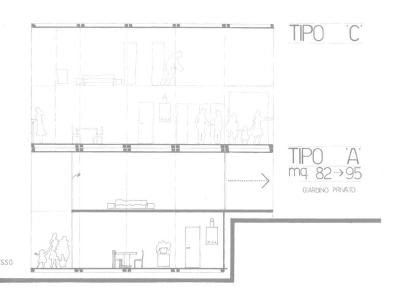

TIPO 'C'

TIPO 'A'
mq. 82→95

GIARDINO PRIVATO

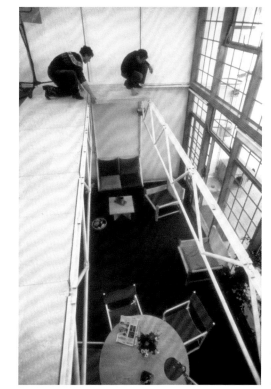

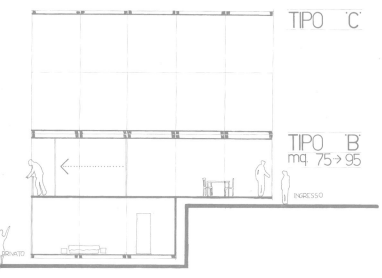

TIPO 'C'

TIPO 'B'
mq. 75→95

INGRESSO

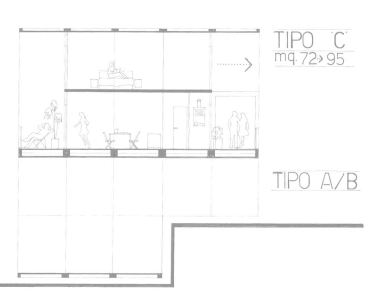

TIPO 'C'
mq. 72→95

TIPO A/B

with large windows, and the internal space could be divided by an intermediate floor supported by a light structural steel framework. This meant that the living area could vary from 50 to 120 metres square, depending on the requirements of the future inhabitants. The home thus created was seen as a 'living organism, imperfect and modifiable', for which the architect supplied only the basic earthquake-proof structure, while the occupants could customize their new homes as desired.[18]

This construction system was extensively adopted, albeit in several variants, in the Il Rigo neighbourhood of Corciano, a town near Perugia.[19] The planning of the complex, consisting of roughly 150 units, was entrusted to the Piano & Rice practice by the Municipality of Corciano, which incorporated the project in its ten-year residential development plan in 1978. Il Rigo was planned by bringing together and superimposing the modules developed for the Friuli competition, connecting them for the most part with pedestrian walkways. The work was preceded by many preliminary meetings between Piano and his colleagues and the future occupants, with a view to clarifying their housing needs and developing a unit that was as functional and efficient as possible.

The structural system adopted was slightly different from the original Evolutive Housing model, being replaced by a tried-and-tested system developed by Vibrocemento Perugia, as the company was then known. Their 2S system was based on the use of prefabricated load-bearing panels for the external walls and ceilings, connected by steel joints. Some of the units, as is evident from the archived drawings, were built using a more traditional system of reinforced concrete uprights and beams, which were cast on the spot, with an infilling of tuff bricks.[20]

Even so, the overall dimensions of the units remained unchanged – 6 x 6 metres for the elevations originally intended to accommodate windows and 12 metres in length – apart from the distribution of internal space, in particular the central bathroom/staircase block, designed to provide rigidity. Where the internal distribution was concerned, in fact, each unit was flexibly subdivided in accordance with one of three different layouts, all of them on two floors.

SOME OF THE COLOURFUL INFILLS THAT DISTINGUISHED THE IL RIGO NEIGHBOURHOOD WHEN FIRST BUILT HAVE SURVIVED TO THIS DAY, FORTY YEARS LATER.

Despite the partial loss of the evolutive character of the units, the Il Rigo project was distinguished by its social implications, thanks to the so-called District Workshop (Laboratorio di quartiere) concept, whereby designers and inhabitants discussed the building methods and together chose and developed the best means of performing the work. Thus the project was carried out collectively and local people actively participated in the decision-making, offering help with the finishing works.[21]

AS USUAL, RENZO PIANO'S
CONSTRUCTION SITES WERE
ORGANIZED AS ENORMOUS
WORKSHOPS FOR ASSEMBLING
COMPONENTS AND PROTOTYPES
THAT HAD FIRST BEEN
PAINSTAKINGLY STUDIED USING
MODELS AND MOCK-UPS.

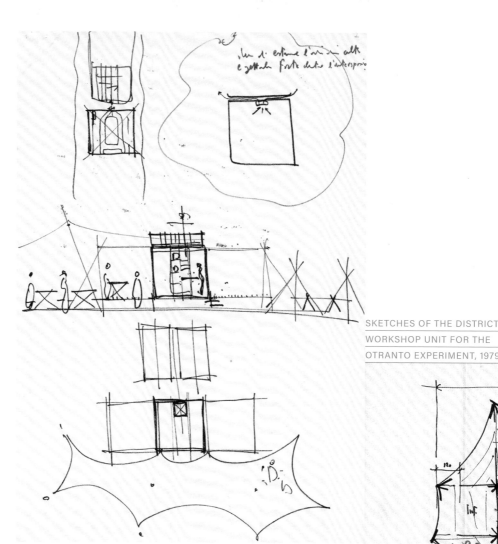

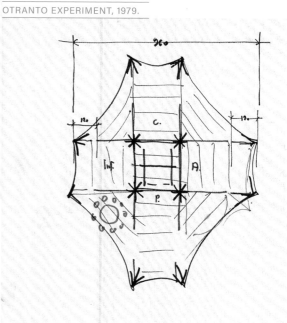

SKETCHES OF THE DISTRICT
WORKSHOP UNIT FOR THE
OTRANTO EXPERIMENT, 1979.

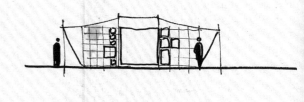

▶ With the District Workshops projects, Piano was aiming for an open and inclusive approach both in the design of individual buildings and in devising strategies for working in urban settings, as demonstrated by the UNESCO-sponsored experiments to renovate the old town centres of Otranto (1979) and Burano (1980).[22]

Piano and his colleagues devised maintenance plans for these neighbourhoods not by undertaking major works but, on the contrary, by going in for 'acupuncture': limited interventions performed after a process of patient scientific analysis, using avant-garde technologies and materials, and with the involvement of the local inhabitants; the locals were not kept at a distance but, on the contrary, invited to participate in the decision-making. These were small-scale interventions, inexpensive and therefore immediately practicable, but capable, if coordinated and shared with the local people, of significantly improving their living conditions – with ongoing maintenance rather than major interventions at widely spaced intervals.[23] The District Workshops experiment was also shaped by Piano's constant methodological imperative: to use the most advanced building materials and techniques, adapting them to small-scale working methods that were intended to imprint on a building, however vast and complex, 'evidence of human handiwork', as Peter Rice liked to put it.[24]

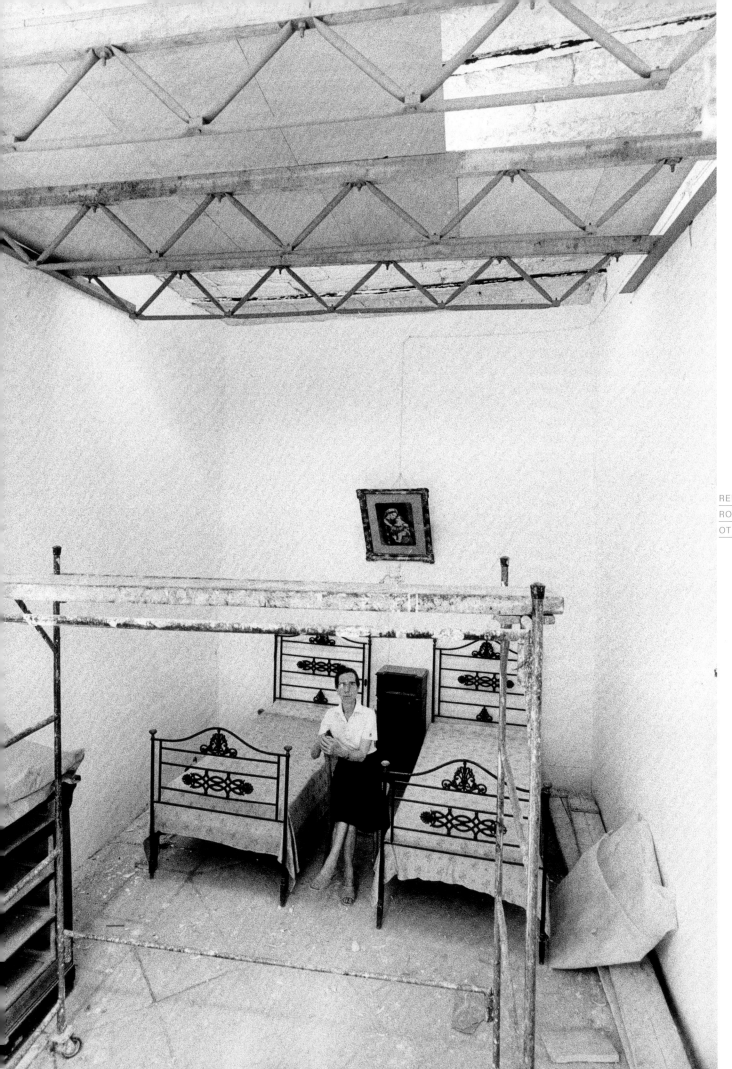

REPLACING THE FLOOR ABOVE IN A
ROOM IN THE HISTORIC CENTRE OF
OTRANTO, 1979.

Again in the District Workshops experiment, the town square and the sharing of time and public space were fundamental principles of Piano's work.

REPAIRING CRACKS: STRUCTURAL AND FUNCTIONAL IMPROVEMENTS WERE THE FOUNDING PRINCIPLE OF THE DISTRICT WORKSHOPS PROJECT.

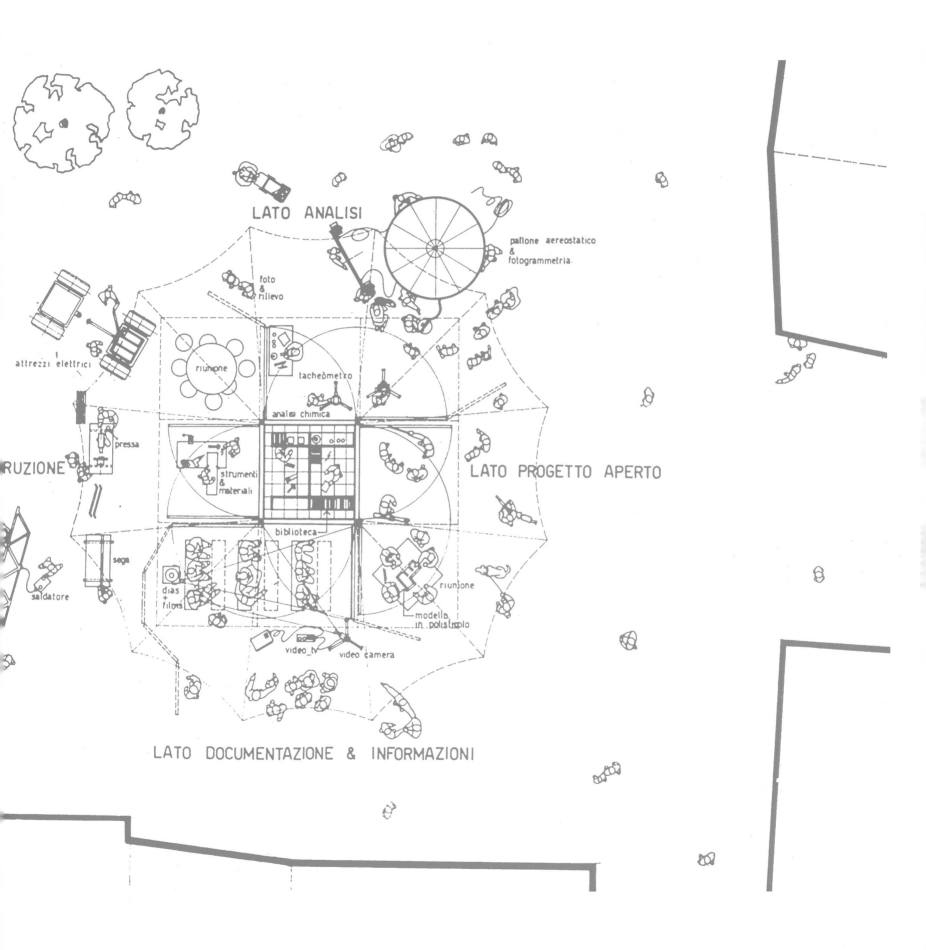

LATO ANALISI

pallone aereostatico
&
fotogrammetria

foto
&
rilievo

tacheòmetro

analisi chimica

riunione

attrezzi elettrici

RUZIONE

pressa

strumenti
&
materiali

LATO PROGETTO APERTO

biblioteca

sega

dias
+
films

saldatore

riunione

modello
in polistirolo

video tv

video camera

LATO DOCUMENTAZIONE & INFORMAZIONI

THE DISTRICT WORKSHOP
UNIT IN THE CASTELLO DI
OTRANTO TOWN SQUARE IN
JUNE 1979.

The District Workshop 'tool' was simply an openable, cube-shaped metal structure that could be assembled in the main square of an old town centre, as in the case of Otranto, making it possible to exhibit panels and create a space sheltered by an awning.[25] The Workshop had four main functions: 'analysis', using diagnostic equipment to perform preliminary checks; 'open project', during which public discussions were held to decide what work should be carried out and how; 'construction', with real live worksite equipment; and, finally, 'documentation and information', whereby the work done was described and catalogued, and an oral record of the local people's impressions made to provide feedback for future projects.

In Otranto, as in Burano, in 1979 and 1980, a number of tasks were performed: damp-proofing of the walls of buildings in the old districts; replacing rotting floors by inserting light, prefabricated structural steelwork; replacing old doors and windows with new ones designed to respect the history and character of the district; developing a system of mobile scaffolding suited to the narrow streets and alleys that would have been inaccessible using conventional construction site equipment.[26]

The District Workshops experiment was particularly significant, not so much for its results as for the development of a method based on listening and openness to the needs of consumers and clients, who were to play a decisive role in the projects that began with the Menil Collection. It also introduced the idea of working in established urban settings by undertaking limited projects designed to stimulate and raise collective awareness of the fate of vast areas of the country – the same praxis as adopted for the projects of the G124, the working groups promoted by Renzo Piano following his appointment as Life Senator of the Italian Republic in 2013.[27]

1 Renzo Piano's eccentric position vis-à-vis the prevailing Italian architectural culture of those years has been pointed out by, among others, Renato Pedio, 'Renzo Piano: itinerario e un primo bilancio', in *L'Architettura. Cronache e Storia*, 313, 1981, pp. 615–617.

2 See Renzo Piano, *Dialoghi di cantiere*, Laterza, Bari 1986, a translation of the original French *Chantier ouvert au public*, Arthaud, Paris 1985.

3 'Lo studio-laboratorio di Renzo Piano a Genova', in *Abitare*, 171, 1979, pp. 18–21.

4 Conversation between the author and Bernard Plattner, Paris, 30 November 2018. See also Lorenzo Ciccarelli, 'Le caméléon à l'écoute: Renzo Piano en France', in Benjamin Chavardès, Federico Ferrari (eds.), *Entre Rome et Las Vegas. La France des années 1980 et la condition postmoderne*, Laboratoire ACS, Paris 2021, pp. 105–117.

5 Conversation between the author and Shunji Ishida, Genoa, 25 May 2021.

6 Peter Rice, 'An Engineer's View', in *Exploring Materials. The Work of Peter Rice*, RIBA, London 1992, p. 3.

7 Peter Rice, 'The Controlled Energy of Renzo Piano', in *Renzo Piano. The Process of Architecture*, 9H Gallery, London 1987, pp. 5–6. See also Peter Rice, *An Engineer Imagines*, Ellipsis, London 1994, pp. 71–80.

8 Renzo Piano 1986, op. cit., pp. 99–111. See also 'Piano in Conversation', in Renzo Piano Building Workshop: 1964–1988, in *a+u*, 3, 1989, p. 18.

9 Peter Rice 1994, op. cit., pp. 135–243. An approach remarked on by Renzo Piano himself, 'Design uguale architettura', in *Casabella*, 484, 1982, pp. 21–23. See the diagrams and drawings conserved at the Renzo Piano Foundation, Projects Archive, Piano & Rice Collection, Fiat VSS experimental car 1978–1980.

10 Jonathan Glancey, 'Piano Pieces', in *The Architectural Review*, 1059, 1983, pp. 60–66.

11 Massimo Dini, *Renzo Piano. Progetti e architetture 1964–1983*, Electa, Milan 1983, pp. 218–223. See also Giulio Macchi, 'Renzo, il Comunicatore', in Carla Garbato, Mario Mastropietro, *Renzo Piano Building Workshop. Exhibit Design*, Lybra, Milan 1992, pp. 5–7.

12 This and the following quotations are taken from the *Habitat* broadcasts in which Renzo Piano featured.

13 Conversation between the author and Shunji Ishida, Genoa, 3 February 2022.

14 A methodological principle to which Piano often referred, for example in Renzo Piano 1986, op. cit., p. 12.

15 Massimo Dini 1983, op. cit., pp. 104–113.

16 De Carlo was possibly the Italian architect to whom Piano was closest in those years, a closeness also fostered by the fact that they were both born in Genoa and that, in 1983, De Carlo returned to Genoa to occupy the chair of Architectural Composition. See Renzo Piano, 'Devo molto a Giancarlo De Carlo', in Margherita Guccione, Alessandra Vittorini (eds.), *Giancarlo De Carlo. Le ragioni dell'architettura*, Electa, Milano 2005, pp. 22–24. See also Alberto Franchini, *Il Villaggio Matteotti a Terni. Giancarlo De Carlo e l'abitare collettivo*, L'Erma di Bretschneider, Rome 2022.

17 See *Costruire e ricostruire. Rassegna di progetti del concorso di idee per la ricostruzione del Friuli*, Associazione Italiana Prefabbricazione, Milan 1978, pp. 174–180; 'Tipologie evolutive', in *Domus*, 583, 1978, pp. 46–48.

18 See 'Esperienze di cantiere. Tre domande a Renzo Piano', in *Casabella*, 439, 1978, p. 42.

19 Following the 1976 competition, the Evolutive Housing prototype was adopted in 1978 for the construction of a housing unit of the same type at Solomeo and a family house at Bastia Umbra. See Carlo Rossi, 'Corciano. Complesso residenziale Il Rigo', in Paolo Belardi, Valeria Menchetelli (eds.), *Da case popolari a case sperimentali*, Fabrizio Fabbri Editore, Perugia 2012, p. 193. See also Renzo Piano Foundation, Projects Archive, Renzo Piano – B.W. Building Workshop Collection, Il Rigo quarter, 1978–1982.

20 Renzo Piano Foundation, Drawings Archive, Room D, Cor_box_001, Cor_003.

21 For the later history of the complex, and the alterations made to the units in response to the occupants' changing requirements, see Lorenzo De Matteis, *Evolutive Housing System di Renzo Piano e Peter Rice*, EAI, 2018.

22 Renzo Piano, Magda Arduino, Mario Fazio, *Antico è bello. Il recupero della città*, Laterza, Bari 1980. See also Renzo Piano 1986, op. cit., pp. 207–222; Luciano Cardellicchio, 'I laboratori di quartiere', in Fulvio Irace (ed.), *Renzo Piano Building Workshop. Le città visibili*, Triennale Electa, Milan 2007, pp. 107–111.

23 See 'La technologie n'est pas toujours industrielle. Une interview de Renzo Piano', in *L'Architecture d'Aujourd'hui*, 212, 1980, pp. 51–54.

24 Peter Rice 1994, op. cit., p. 77.

25 In Otranto the UNESCO-sponsored District Workshops experiment took place over a week, from 12 to 18 June 1979. See Lamberto Rossi, 'Il laboratorio di quartiere' in *Spazio e società*, 8, 1979, pp. 36–38.

26 Massimo Dini 1983, op. cit., pp. 64–73, 172–175.

27 *G124. Renzo Piano. Diario delle periferie/1. Giambellino, Milano 2015*, Skira, Milan 2016.

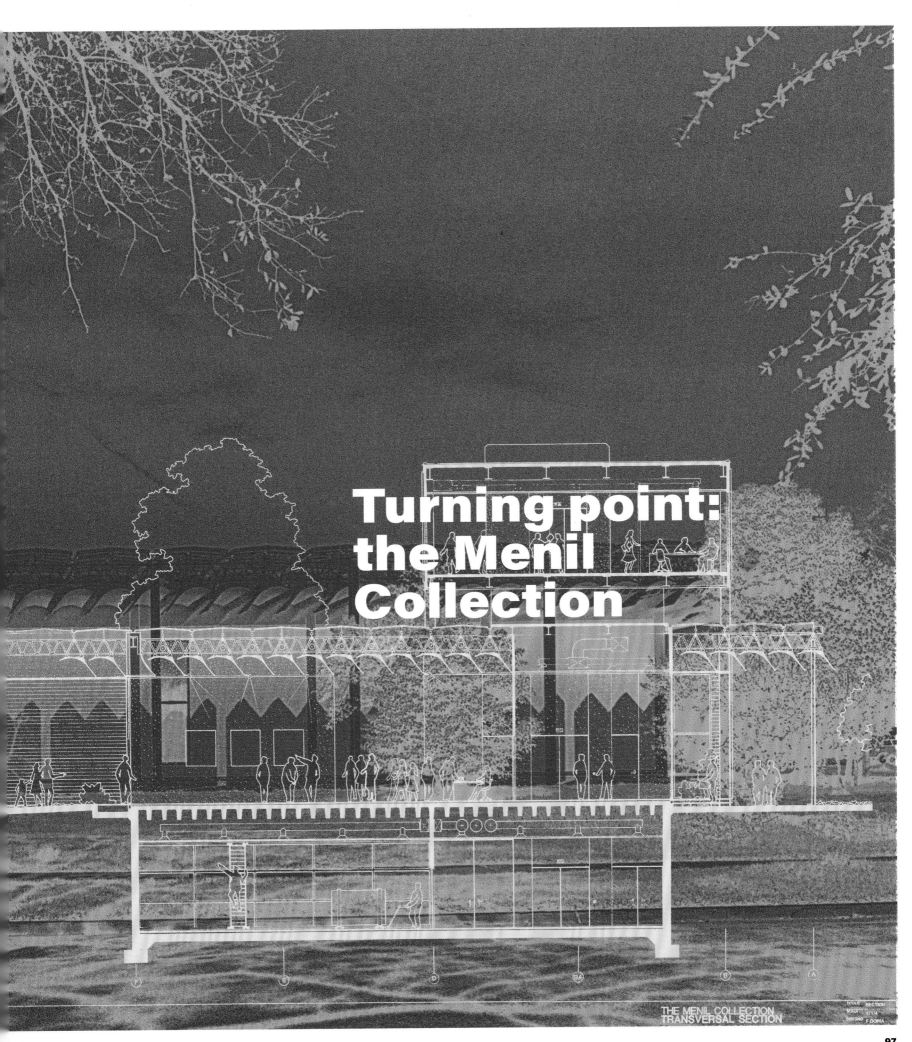

Turning point:
the Menil
Collection

THE MENIL COLLECTION
TRANSVERSAL SECTION

In 2007 Renzo Piano returned to Houston to give a speech commemorating the twentieth anniversary of the opening of the Menil Collection (1981–1986). It was a time of great promise for the Renzo Piano Building Workshop, which had just been commissioned to design an extension to the Kimbell Art Museum in Fort Worth (2007–2013) and new premises for the Whitney Museum of American Art in New York (2007–2015). Piano was also working on enlargements to the Isabella Stewart Gardner Museum in Boston (2005–2012), the Harvard Art Museum (2006–2014), the Art Institute of Chicago (2000–2009) and the Los Angeles County Museum of Art (2003–2010), having previously completed buildings for the Nasher Sculpture Center in Dallas (1999–2003) and the High Museum of Art in Atlanta (1999–2005). So, an impressive and unprecedented series of projects, which made Renzo Piano the point of reference for the design of exhibition spaces and cultural centres in the United States.[1]

The glowing reputation he enjoyed was due in large part to the Menil Collection. In this chapter we shall explain how Renzo Piano's meeting with Dominique de Menil (1908–1997) at the beginning of the 1980s was a turning point in his career.[2]

As we have seen, following completion of work on the Pompidou Centre, Piano dissolved his professional partnership with Richard Rogers and returned to Genoa, where with a small group of colleagues he concentrated on experimental projects, having received no further major commissions. It was thanks to the Menil Collection project that in 1981 he was able to establish the Building Workshop, employ some of his most trusted co-workers, recover his international visibility and 'make landfall' on American soil, where in the following decades he was to obtain the majority of his most prestigious commissions.[3] And whereas the Pompidou Centre was a deliberately provocative display of architectural fireworks, it was thanks to his dialogue with Dominique de Menil that Piano developed the approach he was to maintain for his subsequent museum projects, featuring sober geometrical lines, natural lighting and subtle ways of connecting the exhibition galleries with their natural and human environment.[4]

Dominique Schlumberger was the daughter of a Catholic family that had amassed a considerable fortune as owners of the Société de Prospection Électrique, founded in 1926 by her father and uncle. They had patented a new way of detecting oil deposits using electromagnetic waves. Her husband Jean (later John) de Menil (1904–1973) was also an executive of the company, following their marriage in 1931.[5]

During the 1930s the couple began collecting works of art, commissioning paintings from avant-garde artists – such as the portrait of Dominique painted in 1932 by Max Ernst, and acquiring African and Oceanic artefacts while travelling on business.[6] Dominique also developed an enthusiasm for interior decoration, for example engaging the modernist architect Pierre Barbe to refurbish their apartments at the Château de Kolbsheim and in the Rue Las Cases in Paris, where they began hanging the paintings they had acquired.[7]

The collection continued to grow, partly as a result of the mentorship of Father Marie-Alain Couturier, who made the young couple aware of the potential spiritual influence of contemporary art if displayed in an appropriate architectural setting.[8] And when, during World War II, the couple decided to move first to New York then to Houston – where the American office of the Schlumberger company was established, one of Dominique's first decisions was to build a new house.[9] Not just a private residence, but a place in which to receive friends and artists, and 'a mechanism to display' the best works in their collection.[10]

The task was entrusted to Philip Johnson (1906–2005). Although at that time Johnson did not have a

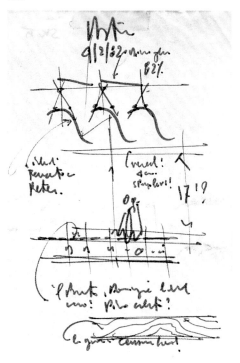

SOME MEMBERS OF THE TEAMS FROM RPBW AND FROM LOCAL ARCHITECT RICHARD FITZGERALD POSING UNDER ONE OF THE FERROCEMENT 'LEAVES' OF THE MENIL COLLECTION.

completed building to his name, he had been an eminent figure at the Museum of Modern Art in New York since 1932, and therefore, in Menil's eyes, was the ideal person to connect the suburbs of Houston with America's most important centre of artistic experimentation. Moreover, because of his lack of experience, Johnson was more likely to be accepting of Dominique de Menil's influence. She had very precise ideas about the domestic space she wanted to occupy and, as with all the later buildings she commissioned, was fully involved in the planning process alongside the architect.

In 1937 Dominique had written two articles for *L'Art Sacré* – the review directed by Marie-Alain Couturier and Maurice Denis devoted to contemporary art and architecture in the context of sacred spaces – concerning a chapel at Kolbsheim and a small church in Japan, articles which reveal the qualities she looked for in a building.

The chapel in the village of Kolbsheim was a modest building, constructed entirely of stone from

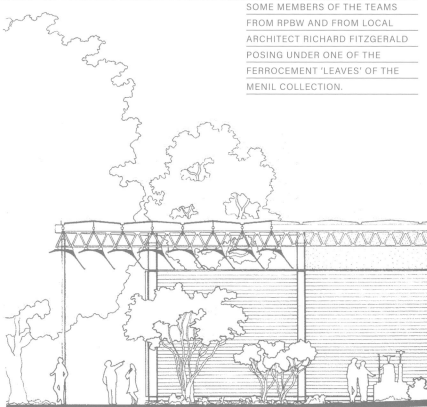

the local quarries. Devoid of any hint of pomp or monumentality, 'une des qualités de cette construction est d'avoir été faite avec de moyens simples et par les artisans du pays... Tout est simple aussi et le charme de cette chapelle provient seulement de l'excellence de ses proportions et de la finesse des détails' ('one of the qualities of this building is that it was created with simple means and by local craftsmen... Everything is simple and the charm of this chapel derives purely from the excellence of its proportions and the delicacy of its details').[11] In contrast with the 'construction faussement audacieuse, où la plus déplorable fantaisie s'allie au plus stérile conformisme' ('bold but bogus approach to

building, in which the most deplorable fantasy is combined with the most sterile conformity'), the interior of the chapel was pervaded with 'sobriété et sensibilité ambiante' ('sobriety and sensitivity to the environment'), the crucifix and tabernacle simply hung on the wall with no superfluous decoration.[12] Similarly, with regard to the little church at Karuizawa, Dominique de Menil appreciated 'la connaissance parfaite des qualités matérielles et spirituelles des matériaux' ('perfect knowledge of the material and spiritual qualities of the materials').[13] The planning of sober, well-proportioned spaces; respect for the character of a place by restricting the height of a building and using local materials;

THE GROUND FLOOR OF THE MENIL COLLECTION IS DEVOTED TO THE EXHIBITION GALLERIES, EDUCATIONAL ACTIVITIES AND RESTORATION WORK, WHILE THE BASEMENT AND FIRST FLOOR HOUSE THE RESERVE COLLECTIONS AND STUDY AREAS.

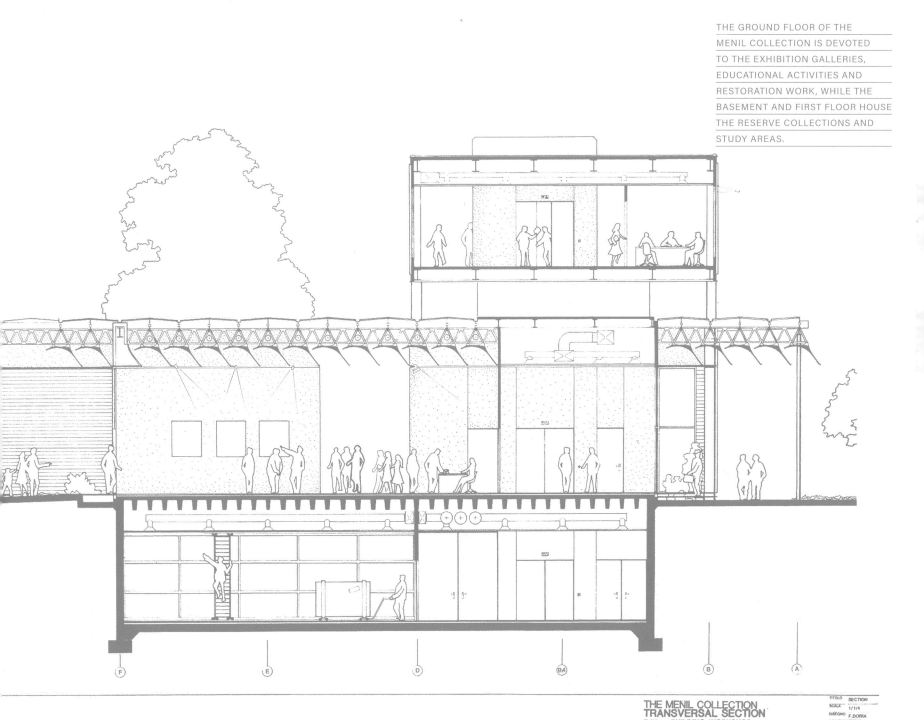

THE MENIL COLLECTION
TRANSVERSAL SECTION
B.W. sm BUILDING WORKSHOP
STUDIO E LABORATORIO DI PROGETTAZIONE
RENZO PIANO   DOTT. ARCH. DIPL. PM. - FAIA
VIALE MODUGNO 22   16156 GENOVA   TEL. 010.68.74.42 · TELEX 222586 PNGBW I

TITOLO   SECTION
SCALA   1/1/4
DISEGNO   F.DORIA
DATA   1.20.84
N:
205 B

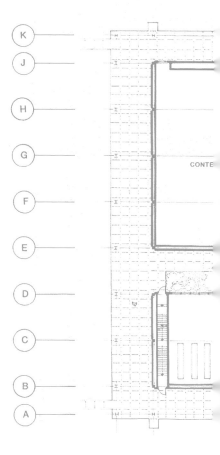

and the elimination of all superfluous decoration were the means envisaged by Dominique de Menil to induce in the visitor a state of 'intimité', the better to approach and contemplate a work of art.[14] The desire to engender this aura of intimacy was the very thing that Dominique de Menil constantly required of 'her' architects, beginning with Philip Johnson.[15]

It may be helpful to stop for a moment and analyse the residence designed by the American architect, since it was the antecedent to which, years later, Piano looked back when conceiving the Menil Collection. Dominique asked Johnson to design a single-storey house, facing north and with a patio at its centre to be adorned with tropical plants that would remind her of the time she had spent with her husband in Venezuela during the war.[16] She also wanted simple flooring of black tiles, and large windows facing onto the garden. The house as built is rectangular in shape, 50 x 21 metres, clad in brick, with a flat roof 3.65 metres in height. The private apartments are at the rear and, revising the initial plan proposed by Johnson, Dominique asked him to do away with the dining room and enlarge the atrium, transforming it into an exhibition space close to the entrance in which to display paintings by Yves Klein, Giorgio de Chirico and René Magritte. Dominique chose not to consult Johnson concerning the furnishings, but entrusted this work to the fashion designer Charles James. She even designed some of the features herself, for instance the octagonal ottoman in the main reception room.[17]

The entrance gallery and main reception room of Menil House were Dominique's first experiments in displaying the works in her collection in an aura of 'intimacy', freely intermixing works of art both antique and contemporary, European and African, with comfortable seating and views of the patio and garden through the spacious windows.

Some thirty years later, Dominique was to make the same demands of Renzo Piano.

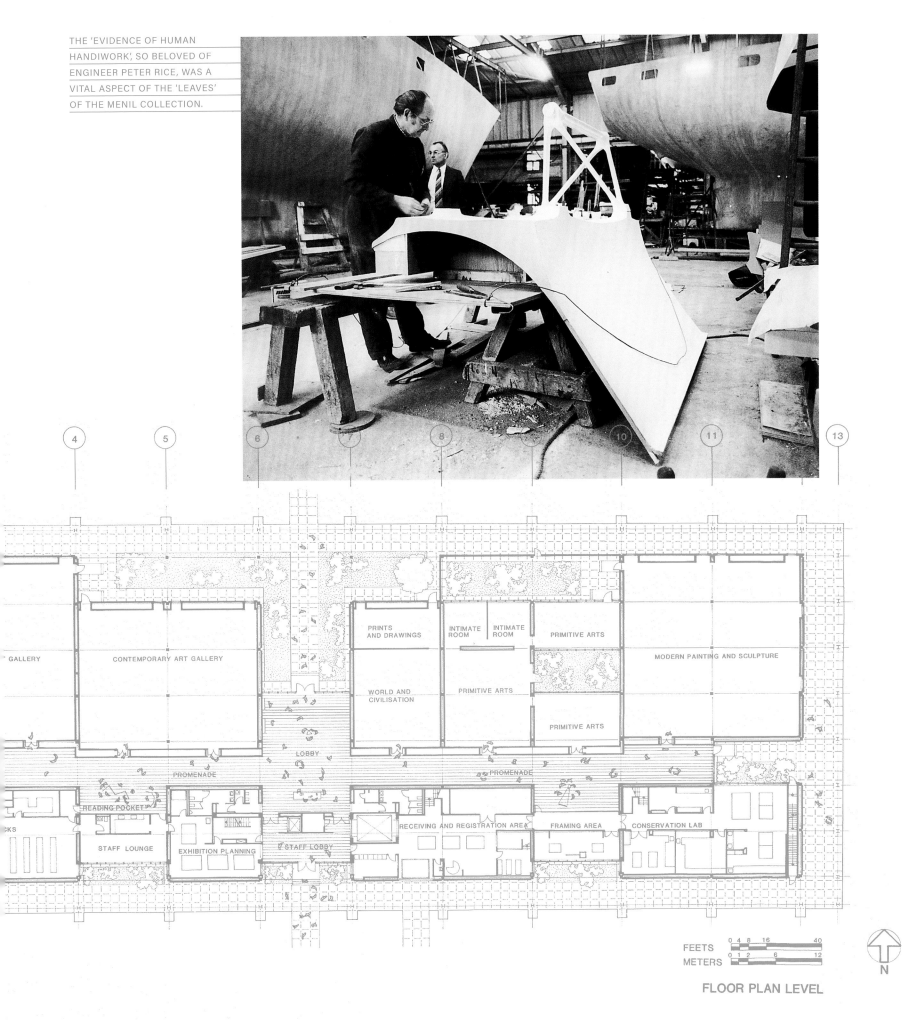

THE 'EVIDENCE OF HUMAN HANDIWORK', SO BELOVED OF ENGINEER PETER RICE, WAS A VITAL ASPECT OF THE 'LEAVES' OF THE MENIL COLLECTION.

GALLERY

CONTEMPORARY ART GALLERY

PRINTS AND DRAWINGS

INTIMATE ROOM

INTIMATE ROOM

PRIMITIVE ARTS

MODERN PAINTING AND SCULPTURE

WORLD AND CIVILISATION

PRIMITIVE ARTS

PRIMITIVE ARTS

LOBBY

PROMENADE

PROMENADE

READING POCKET

RECEIVING AND REGISTRATION AREA

FRAMING AREA

CONSERVATION LAB

STAFF LOUNGE

EXHIBITION PLANNING

STAFF LOBBY

CKS

FEETS 0 4 8 16 40
METERS 0 1 2 6 12

N

FLOOR PLAN LEVEL

THE MENIL COLLECTION MUSEUM MARCH 1987

During their first meeting in Paris in November 1980, she asked for a 'domestic' and 'anti-monumental' museum that must be 'small on the outside and large on the inside.'[18]

It was Pontus Hultén (1924–2006), art historian and first director of the Pompidou Centre, who suggested that Dominique de Menil – a member since 1974 of the Centre's acquisitions committee – consult Renzo Piano as an architect likely to listen sympathetically to her requests.[19] And indeed, as with her private residence, Dominique had some very specific ideas for the museum she had in mind.

The project for a place in which to display the works of the Menil Collection dates back to the early 1970s, when an initial commission awarded to American architect Louis Kahn came to nothing following his death in 1974, and that of John de Menil a year later.[20] At the time of the design and building of Menil House, Dominique had been a young woman and tyro art lover, but in the years that followed she had gained a great deal of experience, succeeding Jermayne MacAgy as director of the Contemporary Arts Association of Houston in 1964 and curating a large number of exhibitions.[21]

To organize the Menil Collection project, Dominique brought together a group of experts that included the future director Paul Winkler and Walter Hopps, who drew up a detailed memorandum. Their report, which contained details of all the museum areas, their dimensions, positions on the plan and internal lighting conditions, was delivered to Dominique de Menil in January 1980, whereas Piano was not contacted until November of that year.[22]

When Piano first travelled to Houston in January 1981, Dominique insisted on hosting him in her own home.[23] And for their meetings in the months that followed Piano continued to stay at Menil House. In discussing the museum, Dominique wanted Piano to breathe the atmosphere she had created in her domestic environment, among artefacts that would later be displayed in the Menil Collection.[24] Dominique explained to Piano that, as she had with Philip Johnson, she wanted

PIANO CAREFULLY PLANNED THE
VOLUMES AND MATERIALS OF THE MENIL
COLLECTION SO THAT THE NEW BUILDING
WOULD FIT SEAMLESSLY AND 'SILENTLY'
INTO THE RESIDENTIAL SUBURB
OF MONTROSE.

to play an active role in designing the museum and, although the architect would have maximum freedom of action in the general planning of the building, she would have the last word on how the galleries were fitted out.[25]

Dominique, who was not an admirer of the Pompidou Centre, asked Piano to respect the fragile balance of the suburb in which the Menil Collection was to be located. The local environment consisted entirely of one- or two-storey residential buildings which she had gradually purchased to house the museum's auxiliary functions.[26] She wanted a building that was sober, horizontal in its lines, with dark floors and natural lighting. She did not intend to incorporate a bookshop or cafeteria in the main building, nor did she want explanatory texts on the walls; every work was to be accompanied simply by the name of the artist, the title, the materials used and the year in which it was created. Moreover, there were to be no physical barriers placed in front of the works of art.[27] Piano must eschew a monumental entrance hall and the foyer must feature neither the name of the museum nor those of any future donors. Dominique de Menil required the same 'domestic' proportions, the same external sobriety and internal 'intimacy' as characterized in her own residence, and the galleries of the Menil Collection must look out onto the same luxuriant patios.[28]

Piano was a good listener and met Dominique de Menil's requirements by designing a two-storey rectangular building: on the ground floor are located the exhibition galleries, the library and the conservation and restoration workshop; on the first floor the so-called 'treasure house', the storage area in which the greater part of the collection is kept in perfect conditions of

THE MENIL COLLECTION IS JUST A STONE'S THROW FROM THE CY TWOMBLY PAVILION, VISIBLE IN THE BOTTOM PART OF THE SITE PLAN ON THE RIGHT, ALSO DESIGNED BY RPBW (1992–1995).

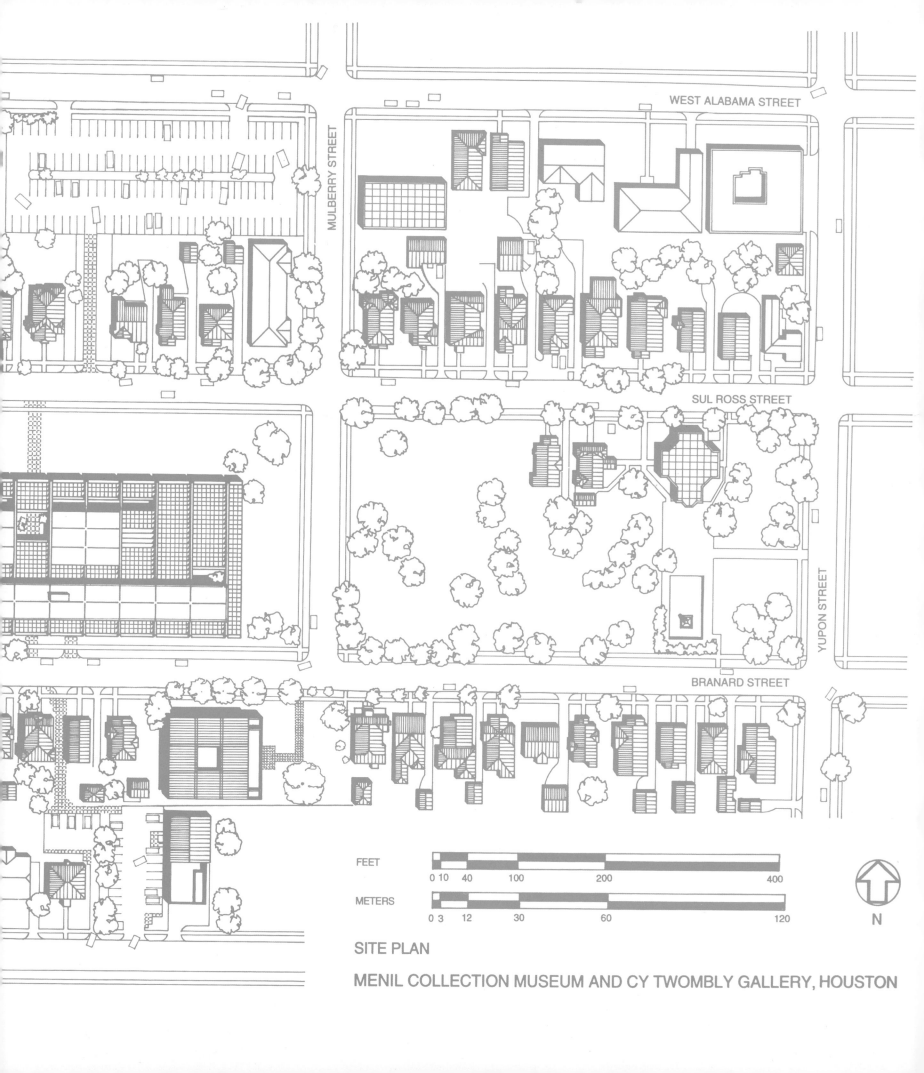

WEST ALABAMA STREET

MULBERRY STREET

SUL ROSS STREET

YUPON STREET

BRANARD STREET

FEET

0 10   40   100   200   400

METERS

0 3   12   30   60   120

N

SITE PLAN

MENIL COLLECTION MUSEUM AND CY TWOMBLY GALLERY, HOUSTON

lighting and humidity.[29] Structurally, the building has a white-painted metal frame infilled with walls made from planks of Louisiana cypress, treated with the same light-grey finish as the surrounding bungalows.

A tripartite area of glazing dividing the main elevation into two equal parts introduces the visitor not into a conventional museum atrium but into a more spacious version of the entrance gallery of Menil House. To emphasize the connection between the two buildings, Dominique de Menil suggested that the flooring be of a similar dark colour – in this case of pinewood planks – and designed a new version of the ottoman that graced her own house. In the Menil Collection entrance hall there are neither information points nor a ticket office, cloakroom or bookshop. As if entering the collector's own home, the visitor is immediately engaged by the works of art: two works by Barnett Newman, *Now II* (1967) and *Anna's Light* (1968), and two sculptures originating from the Congo.[30]

This entrance gallery is delimited by a corridor that runs crossways through the building, creating two separate wings. On the northern side are six galleries: two larger ones devoted to Western art of the 19th and 20th centuries to the left of the entrance, and a vast room for modern painting and sculpture, flanked on the right by two areas reserved for primitive and Oceanic art. On the southern side of the corridor are the library, study rooms and the conservation and restoration workshop. At Dominique de Menil's express request, these work areas were accorded the same dignity as the exhibition galleries, with large windows to encourage curious passers-by to look in on the work of the museum staff.[31]

To reinforce the 'intimacy' of the Menil Collection, all the services and technical installations were confined to an 'energy room' located on the south side of the site, beyond some of the bungalows, and connected to the museum by underground ducting. Nothing was to distract visitors from contemplation of the works of art.

The plan of the Menil Collection is punctuated by a series of patios and gardens. At the end of the central corridor, two small gardens interrupt the profile of the building, while three green areas are laid out along the rear elevation – in front of the restoration workshop and the staff entrance, and close to the atrium on the entrance side. Finally, between the galleries of primitive and Oceanic art there is a small patio adorned with the same tropical vegetation as that of Menil House.

Piano and his colleagues spent a long time considering the best way to filter natural light into the exhibition galleries as requested by Dominique de Menil, who had already experienced the delicate modulation of solar radiation during construction of the Rothko Chapel (1964–1971), on a site not far from where the new museum was to be built.[32]

BELOW: INTRADOS OF THE MUSEUM'S
ROOFING STRUCTURE, CLEARLY SHOWING
THE FERROCEMENT 'LEAVES.'
OPPOSITE: THE FERROCEMENT LEAVES
AND ONE OF THE RETICULAR BEAMS
MADE OF SPHEROID CAST IRON TO WHICH
THE LEAVES ARE ATTACHED.

The Menil Collection ensured Renzo Piano's reputation as an architect of sober and precisely calculated exhibition areas characterized by natural lighting and respectful integration of buildings with their natural settings.

Mark Rothko's studio in New York featured a large central skylight so that he could paint and observe his canvases in natural light, and he could modulate this by using blinds.[33] When in 1964 John and Dominique de Menil invited Rothko to produce ten monumental paintings to adorn the walls of a new ecumenical chapel they wanted to build in Houston, Rothko asked to be involved in the architectural planning, making it a condition that his works be lit exclusively by natural light. For this reason both the initial design by Philip Johnson and the final one by Howard Barnstone and Eugene Aubry featured a large steel-and-glass octagonal skylight/lantern. However, after the chapel was inaugurated they realized that, modulated in this way, the intense light of Texas was too strong for Rothko's paintings, and so a diffuser was hung from the lantern to partially screen the sun's rays.

Piano visited the Rothko Chapel with Dominique de Menil during his first visit to Houston in 1981 and also studied the roofing systems of Louis Kahn's Kimbell Art Museum, not far away. Advised by Pontus Hultén,

THE GALLERY DEVOTED TO
OCEANIC SCULPTURE, WITH
THE CENTRAL PATIO AND
ITS LUXURIANT TROPICAL
VEGETATION IN THE
BACKGROUND.

Piano and Dominique de Menil went to see a small museum on the Ein Harod kibbutz in Israel, where the galleries were naturally lit using a similar system of monolithic diffusers under a continuous series of skylights.[34]

Piano adopted a different strategy for his roofing structures, revisiting the prefabricated components he had experimented with in the 1960s. In collaboration with engineers Peter Rice and Tom Barker, he decided to break up the roof of the museum into a series of superimposed layers, designing a *pezzo* that could be mass-produced and assembled dry on site.[35] The famous three hundred ferrocement 'leaves' form the lower layer of the Menil Collection roof, attached to spheroidal cast-iron beams that also support the glazed panels positioned above them.[36]

In designing the roof structure, Piano was concerned not only with protection from or modulation of light – it also represented his stylistic signature as an architect. It is no coincidence that the ferrocement leaves are not positioned on the outside of the shell – as would be the case with a traditional canopy – but on the inside, beneath the skylights, so that visitors can see them when walking around the building or from inside the galleries.[37] Reactions to the Menil Collection were extremely positive. The critics praised the 'domestic scale' of the building and its 'unpretentious' character.[38] Unlike the Pompidou Centre, the Menil Collection seemed to 'draw its strength from its concept rather than the memorability of its form'.[39] And Reyner Banham, who visited the worksite on several occasions, wrote of 'a structure that doesn't even try to look like a museum', having an aura of 'ethereal beauty'.[40]

The Swiss collector Ernst Beyeler was so impressed by the Menil Collection that a few years later he asked Piano to design a similar building (1991–1997) to house his collection in Basel. And the same was true of the ultra-wealthy Raymond Nasher, for whom the Renzo Piano Building Workshop designed an exhibition centre for sculpture in Dallas, in both cases following the strategy developed in Houston: linear layout, blind walls along streets and large areas of glass overlooking internal patios and courtyards, together with 'leafed' roof structures designed to modulate the degree of natural light required by the works on show.

Dominique de Menil's vision – the aura of 'intimacy' to be conveyed by the exhibition space and the primacy of the works of art over any architectural fireworks – completely reversed Piano's public image as determined by the Pompidou Centre.[41]

Whereas the great American museums completed in the 1980s – Richard Meier's High Museum of Art in Atlanta (1980–1983) or Arata Isozaki's Museum of Contemporary Art in Los Angeles (1980–1986) – were characterized by attractive photogenic shapes and monumental foyers and public areas, Piano offered an alternative approach characterized by natural light, well-proportioned galleries and inclusion of the urban setting in the museum space. In the following decades this approach was to earn him considerable credit and many commissions.

The content of this chapter is a rewrite of an earlier article of mine: Lorenzo Ciccarelli, 'Renzo Piano, Dominique de Menil and the Artifice of Intimacy', in *Art Collections 2020. Design and Museum Design, Digital Heritage, Historical Research* – conference proceedings (Florence, University of Florence, 21–23 September 2020), edited by Francesco Valerio Collotti, Giorgio Verdiani, Alessandro Brodini, Didapress, Florence 2020, pp. 317–326.

[1] Federico Bucci, 'In the Age of Piano', in *Casabella*, 797, 2011, pp. 69–70.

[2] See Lia Piano (ed.), *Menil Collection*, Renzo Piano Foundation, Genoa 2007. The decisive role that Dominique de Menil played in the design of the museum was commented on by Piano himself in *Il mestiere di architetto*, Cluva, Venice 1984, pp. 63, 68.

[3] For example, Mark Carroll, now an RPBW Partner, was taken on precisely for the Menil Collection project: See Mark Carroll, 'L'età dell'innocenza', in *Abitare*, 497, 2009, pp. 134–135.

[4] See Victoria Newhouse, *Renzo Piano Museums*, The Monacelli Press, New York 2007.

[5] William Middleton, *Double Vision. The Unerring Eye of Art World Avatars Dominique and John de Menil*, Alfred Knopf, New York 2018, pp. 84–87, 193–194.

[6] Kristina van Dyke, 'Losing One's Head: John and Dominique de Menil as Collectors', in Josef Helfenstein, Laureen Schipse (eds.), *Art and Activism. Projects of John and Dominique de Menil*, The Menil Collection/ Yale University Press, Houston/New Haven and London 2010, pp. 119–137.

[7] Jean-Baptiste Minnaert, *Pierre Barbe architecte*, Mardaga, Liège 1991.

[8] William Middleton 2018, op. cit., pp. 185–187; Antoine Lion (ed.), *Marie-Alain Couturier. Un Combat Pour L'Art Sacré*, Editions du Cerf, Nice 2005.

[9] William Middleton 2018, op. cit., pp. 327–350.

[10] Bruce Webb, 'Living Modern in Mid-Century Houston: Conserving the Menil House', in *Journal of Architectural Education*, 1, 2008, pp. 11–19; Jesus Vassallo, 'Doll's House', in *AA Files*, 70, 2015, pp. 19–23.

[11] Dominique de Menil, 'Remarques sur une chapelle', in *L'Art Sacré*, 17, 1937, pp. 90–91.

[12] Ibid., p. 91.

[13] Dominique de Menil, 'Leçon d'une chapelle japonais', in *L'Art Sacré*, 18, 1937, pp. 117–119.

[14] Dominique de Menil 1937, op. cit., p. 91.

[15] Frank Welch, *Philip Johnson & Texas*, University of Texas Press, Austin 2000; Pamela Smart, *Sacred Modern. Faith, Activism and Aesthetics in the Menil Collection*, University of Texas Press, Austin 2010.

[16] Steve Fox, 'Dominique and John de Menil as Patrons for Architecture', in Josef Helfenstein, Laureen Schipse (eds.) 2010, op. cit., pp. 199–217.

[17] Controversial decisions that led Johnson to consider the de Menils' residence as not entirely his own work.

[18] Renzo Piano, 'Working with Light: A Portrait of Dominique de Menil', in Josef Helfenstein, Laureen Schipse (eds.) 2010, op. cit., p. 218.

[19] 'Du Musée national d'art moderne à la collection de Menil'. Interview with Pontus Hultén, in Luciana Miotto (ed.), *Renzo Piano*, Editions du Centre Pompidou, Paris 1987, pp. 70–71.

[20] Patricia Loud, *The Art Museums of Louis I. Kahn*, Duke University Press, Durham 1989.

[21] Pamela Smart, 'Aesthetic as Vocation', in Josef Helfenstein, Laureen Schipse (eds.) 2010, op. cit., pp. 26–27.

[22] The report is conserved at the Renzo Piano Foundation, Documents Archive, Menil, Pfitz/MEN/001.

[23] Shunji Ishida, 'Towards an Invisible Light: Design Development', in *a+u*, 11, 1987, pp. 64–70.

[24] Walter Hopps, *La rime et la raison. Les collections Menil Houston-New York*, Galeries Nationales du Grand Palais, Paris 1984.

[25] William Middleton 2018, op. cit., p. 585.

[26] Ibid., p. 575.

[27] Ibid., p. 4. See also Pamela Smart 2010, op. cit., p. 27.

[28] Dominique de Menil, 'The Menil Collection and Museum', in *a+u*, 11, 1987, p. 62.

[29] Piano's ability to listen and his exhaustive dialogue with Dominique de Menil are recalled by Paul Winkler, 'Being a Client', in *Renzo Piano. The Art of Making Buildings*, Royal Academy of Arts, London 2018, p. 129. The archive drawings are conserved at the Renzo Piano Foundation, Projects Archive, Piano & Fitzgerald Collection, The Menil Collection 1980–1987.

[30] William Middleton 2018, op. cit., pp. 17–18.

[31] Shunji Ishida 1987, op. cit., p. 67.

[32] Dominique de Menil, 'The Rothko Chapel', in *The Art Journal*, 3, 1970, pp. 249–251; Susan Barnes, *The Rothko Chapel. An Act of Faith*, University of Texas Press, Austin 1989; Ryan Dohoney, *Saving Abstraction: Morton Feldman, the de Menils and the Rothko Chapel*, Oxford University Press, Oxford 2019.

[33] William Middleton 2018, op. cit., p. 478.

[34] Paul Winkler 2018, op. cit., pp. 124–125.

[35] Conversation between the author and Mark Carroll, Genoa, 31 July 2020. The structure of the Menil Collection roof is discussed in detail by Tom Barker, Alistair Guthrie, Neil Noble, Peter Rice, 'The Menil Collection', in *The Arup Journal*, 1, 1983, pp. 2–7.

[36] See Francesco Dal Co, *Renzo Piano*, Electa, Milan 2014, pp. 154–155.

[37] Richard Ingersoll, 'The Porosity of the Menil Collection', in Josef Helfenstein, Laureen Schipse (eds.) 2010, op. cit., p. 227. See also Edgar Stach, Renzo Piano Building Workshop. *Space-Detail-Light*, Birkhäuser, Basel 2021, pp. 20–30.

[38] See Jonathan Glancey, 'Piano Pieces', in *The Architectural Review*, 1059, 1983, pp. 59–63; Peter Davey, 'Menil Museum', in *The Architectural Review*, 1081, 1987, pp. 36–42.

[39] Richard Ingersoll, 'Pianissimo: The Very Quiet Collection', in *Texas Architects*, 3, 1987, pp. 40–47.

[40] Reyner Banham, 'In the Neighborhood of Art', in *Art in America* 6, 1987, pp. 124–129.

[41] See Reyner Banham, 'Making Architecture: The High Craft of Renzo Piano, in Renzo Piano Building Workshop: 1964–1988', in *a+u*, 3, 1989, pp. 155–156.

Scaling up: Osaka and Berlin

Whereas in 1986, when the Menil Collection was inaugurated, the Renzo Piano Building Workshop numbered a mere thirty or so co-workers engaged on small- and medium-scale projects just in Italy and France, by the year 2000 the practice consisted of around 1,500 people, working on projects in the United States, the Netherlands, Switzerland, Germany, Japan, Australia and New Caledonia. And by then Renzo Piano had been awarded the Pritzker Architecture Prize (1998) and a Golden Lion for his life's work at the Venice Biennale (2000).

The 1990s were decisive for the growth and international affirmation of both Renzo Piano and the Building Workshop: a golden age which we shall cover in this chapter and the next. We shall focus in particular on the two projects that triggered this process of scaling up: the Kansai Airport terminal in Osaka (1988–1994) and the reconstruction of the Potsdamer Platz area of Berlin (1992–2000). At the same time, we shall analyse the changes in the organizational and managerial structure of the practice that this growth necessitated and, in the next chapter, examine a second series of projects in which Piano's 'traditional' experimentation with construction techniques and materials was accompanied by closer attention to the public nature of architecture and its settings. For the Building Workshop, these 1990s projects forged a concept of architecture as the art and technique of building and as a driving force in fostering social relations, and sparked off its more recent productions.[1]

Although Renzo Piano had already tackled the complicated task of planning and constructing the Pompidou Centre, the Kansai Airport terminal and the reconstruction of the Potsdamer Platz area were still quite unprecedented challenges in terms of scale and complexity. For example, the surface area of the Paris cultural centre is 7,500 metres square, that of Kansai Airport almost 300,000. And on this project the Renzo Piano Building Workshop

was heading up – and had to manage and integrate – an international consortium of architectural practices and planning offices.[2]

▶ The new terminal at Kansai International Airport is a manifesto of Renzo Piano's poetics and was a turning point in the development of the Building Workshop. It was the last project on which Piano worked closely with his associate Noriaki Okabe and with his engineer friends from Ove Arup & Partners, Peter Rice and Tom Barker. It was also the commission that enabled him to double both his staff and the space available to him in the Piazza San Matteo studio in central Genoa and, from 1992, in his new premises on the slopes of the Punta Nave hill at Vesima.[3] But above all it was the clearest demonstration of a working method in which mastery of materials and building techniques, and the availability of new computing tools, were used not to shape a stunning edifice, but to integrate and systematize the many degrees of complexity involved in a large-scale building within a straightforward, essential and immediately comprehensible architectural form. For Renzo Piano the success of an architectural project lies not in the complex organization of space nor in formal artificiality, but in the fact that the form in question is the logical result of rigorous integration of the client's requirements and the structural, technical and performance-related demands it entails. As he sees it, technology is the fundamental tool for drawing everything together in a unified vision and making this miracle possible.

In the early 1970s the Japanese central government and the Kansai region began planning the enlargement of the airport at Osaka, centre of one of the country's most vibrant industrial and technological areas. After long deliberations, they decided to build the new international terminal on an artificial island in Osaka Bay, 5 kilometres

ONE OF RENZO PIANO'S FIRST
SKETCHES SHOWS THE HIGH ROOF
FORMING A SPACIOUS CHANNEL
LEADING TO THE GATES AND
EMBARKATION AREAS.

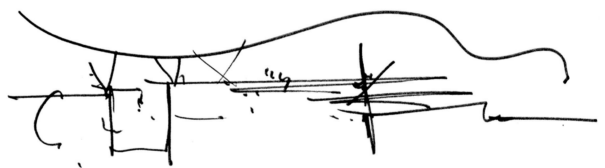

FROM THE START THE IDEA WAS TO
BRING THE DIFFERENT PARTS OF
THE TERMINAL TOGETHER UNDER
A LARGE AERODYNAMIC ROOF.

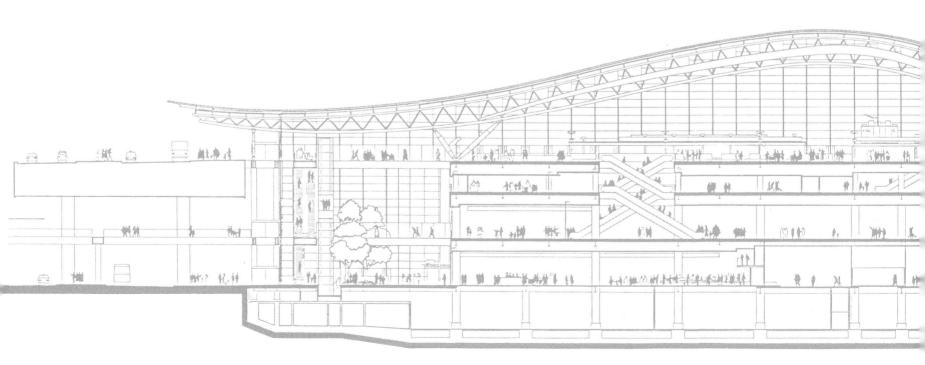

from the coast and 40 kilometres south-east of the city.[4] Creating the island – a 4.37 x 1.25-kilometre platform – was a colossal work of engineering managed by the Japanese authorities, in which neither the Renzo Piano Building Workshop nor Ove Arup & Partners were involved. Meanwhile, the Kansai International Airport Company (commissioning authority and final customer) invited six of the largest Japanese architectural practices to propose plans for the new terminal, which was to accommodate both domestic and international flights, with the ambition of becoming a major hub for air traffic in the Pacific and South-Asian region. The preferred design – proposed by Nikken Sekkei – was shared by the client with several of the world's main airport authorities, with the aim of garnering further opinions and suggestions before going ahead with the massive investment involved. The most surprising reply was received from Aéroport de Paris, the company that managed the airports in the Île de France region. Aéroport de Paris's planning office specializing in transport infrastructure was run by Paul Andreu, and he drew up a completely new scheme for the Kansai terminal. He broke with the traditional system of having separate terminals for domestic and international flights, bringing them together on different levels within the same building, from either end of which long 'wings' led to the passenger embarkation points.[5] This solution – now routine but innovative at the time – so convinced the Kansai International Airport Company that they decided not to go ahead with Nikken Sekkei. Instead they engaged Aéroport de Paris as the lead consultant in the consortium they were putting together and launched an international competition, inviting major

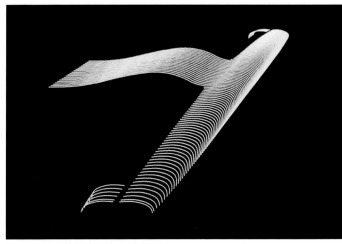

THE COMPUTER MODEL FOR THE DIFFERENT RADII OF CURVATURE OF THE TERMINAL ROOF.

A CROSS-SECTIONAL VIEW OF THE KANSAI INTERNATIONAL AIRPORT TERMINAL SHOWING, FROM LEFT TO RIGHT, THE ENTRANCE, THE RETAIL AND SECURITY-CHECK AREAS, THE GATES AND THE EMBARKATION AREAS.

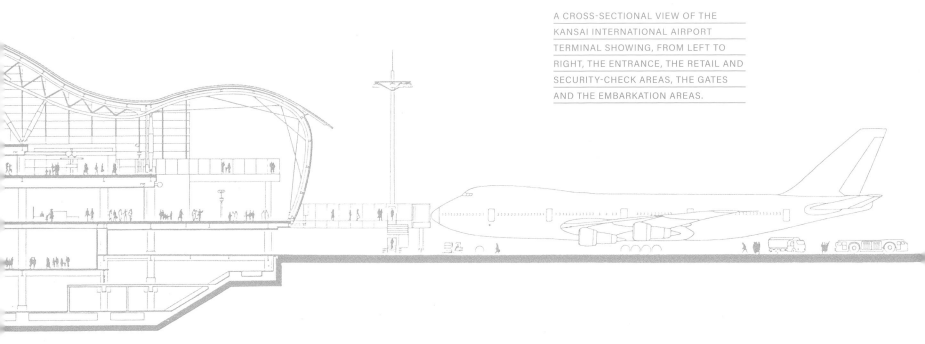

Work on the mammoth Kansai International Airport project lasted 38 months, employing up to 10,000 people working in perfect coordination.

architectural practices to participate whether or not they had experience in designing airport terminals, thus including the Renzo Piano Building Workshop.[6]

The person who convinced a hesitant Renzo Piano to participate in the competition was Noriaki Okabe, his close collaborator since 1974, and he took the lead as project manager of the Kansai adventure. To supervise the most intense phases of planning and construction, he opened and coordinated the Building Workshop office in Osaka and in 1995, once the terminal was inaugurated, left to establish an independent practice in Tokyo. Renzo Piano decided to involve Peter Rice and Tom Barker, as well as Okabe, from the time of the first site inspections.

The designers made a first visit to Osaka Bay in September 1988, out at sea in a small boat, and their first impressions were of the wind whipping up the waves and the Ōmine mountain range in the distance, visible beyond the coastline and city. Piano was persuaded that the new terminal should have a strong presence in the landscape, lest it be overwhelmed by the majesty of the bay and mountain chain, and should have as unitary and aerodynamic a form as possible to brave the wind and the waves breaking on the artificial island.

Piano and Okabe did not deviate from the overall layout proposed by Aéroport de Paris.[7] The four-level central body of the

A SPECTACULAR IMAGE OF THE MASSIVE CURVED GIRDERS BEING ASSEMBLED ON THE OSAKA WORKSITE.

terminal is organized as follows – top floor: international departures; first floor: shops, offices and accessory premises; ground floor: domestic departures and arrivals; below-ground level: international arrivals. On the western side of this parallelepiped structure are the railway station and the access roads, while on the eastern side are the domestic-flight embarkation areas. Meanwhile, the two lateral wings, 1.7 kilometres in length, serve the international flight gates.

Despite the modifications and many adaptations imposed by the budget, and the ongoing development of the project during the six years between the competition and the inauguration of the terminal, the essential principle of Piano, Okabe, Rice and Barker's design remained unchanged: the general layout, the load-bearing structure, the technical services and the shape of the shell must be systematized and integrated so as to make

movement within the enormous structure as simple and intuitive as possible.

Passengers first enter a large area three storeys high – nicknamed 'the canyon' – on the western side of the terminal. Here they can immediately form a clear picture of the different floors of the airport and their specific functions, before travelling via escalators and lifts to the level and area where they need to be. They simply move through the central body of the terminal, with no need to exit and re-enter different parts of the airport. Once departing passengers have passed through security and reached the eastern side of the terminal, a series of shuttles transports them along one of the wings to the appropriate gate. The shape of the roof and its supporting structure plainly indicate the direction of flow. An undulating metal ribbon runs right through the terminal, at its widest in the centre of the building and at its narrowest at the extremities. As a result, passengers in the canyon are directed, by the height of the roof and the intensity of the light, to move through the terminal towards the security-check area and the gates. Similarly, the roofline gradually reduces as passengers travel along the wings towards their end points, ushering

CLEARLY VISIBLE: THE DOUBLE
CURVE OF THE ROOF OF THE
KANSAI INTERNATIONAL AIRPORT
TERMINAL IN OSAKA BAY.

RENZO PIANO AND PETER RICE
WORKING ON THE PLANS FOR
KANSAI IN THE TEMPORARY STUDIO
OPENED IN OSAKA FOR THE
DURATION OF THE PROJECT, 1990.

them from the central building to the embarkation areas. The metal structure supporting the roof – asymmetrical reticular girders 80 metres in length resting on enormous inverted four-armed trestles supported by circular-section pillars – forms a sinuous channel from the canyon to the departure gates, also serving to indicate the direction of flow.

The complex shape of the roofs – a unidirectional curved surface for the terminal building, obtained by joining portions of cylinders of differing radii tangentially; and a toroidal-shaped bidimensional curved surface for the two wings, obtained by welding portions of rotating surfaces of different radius – was the result of patient and sophisticated calculations by Peter Rice, Tom Barker and the Ove Arup & Partners engineers, working in close contact with Piano, Okabe and the Building Workshop team.[8]

The shape of the roof has numerous advantages: all planes landing and taking off from the airport are visible from the control tower with the naked eye; passengers inside the terminal can see the planes at the different gates through the glazed screens on either side of the building, making it easier for them to find their way around; all of the 82,000 steel roof panels are of the same standard size, driving down the cost of construction and simplifying assembly operations. Moreover, the curvilinear shape of the roof, and the fact that it extends uninterrupted over the whole length and breadth of the terminal, makes it easier to channel and distribute fresh air efficiently, without the cumbersome

THE ENTRANCE 'CANYON' TO THE TERMINAL AND THE EMBARKATION GALLERY, SHOWING THE SHEER HEIGHT OF THESE AREAS.

ducting that would normally be visible or concealed by false ceilings.[9] A series of baffles facilitates air movement, giving airport users an unobstructed view of the load-bearing structure and the underside of the roof, and revealing its fluid geometry to them. Being completely exposed, the load-bearing structure – as with the Pompidou Centre – has aesthetic value and mediates between the sheer size of the terminal and the human activity for which it was designed.

Without the processing power of personal computers – which in those years were beginning to be essential tools for architects and engineers, it would not have been possible to realize the roof of Kansai Airport as planned. However, and this was to become a characteristic of the working method of the Building Workshop, the freedom afforded by computers was not used to create pointlessly spectacular designs as an end in themselves, but rather to make designers more disciplined in integrating form and structure, stereometry and service installations.[10]

Management of the various phases of the Kansai International Airport terminal project also presented the Building Workshop with a considerable challenge. Hitherto the Workshop had tackled only small- and medium-scale projects, in geographical and regulatory contexts similar to those of Italy and France. Although the competition entry was drawn up in the Paris office, Piano decided to transfer the project to Genoa, to the studio in Piazza San Matteo, where since 1988 the

practice had occupied the first floor of the historic *palazzo*. To accommodate the dozens of young architects recruited at this stage, Piano also rented the third floor and, in 1991 and 1992, moved to the new Punta Nave building at Vesima. Noriaki Okabe was despatched to Japan to open and coordinate the practice's new office in Osaka, while Shunji Ishida took charge of the group working in Genoa. The sharing of ideas and project updates meant frequent telephone calls and a continuous exchange of faxed documents between the Italian and Japanese offices of the Building Workshop and with Ove Arup & Partners in London. Meanwhile, weekly and monthly reviews and in-person meetings were organized among the staff of the three offices.[11] The project, which went on for 38 months, employed an average of 6,000 workers each day, sometimes peaking at 10,000. The terminal was completed in June 1994 and opened to air traffic on 4 September of that year, soon achieving the status of regional and international hub for which it had been conceived.

Peter Rice, seriously ill, did not live to see the terminal completed: he died in October 1992. Soon after, Tom Barker left the Ove Arup & Partners' planning division to take on senior management responsibilities. The Kansai Airport terminal, which projected Renzo Piano and the Building Workshop into a new dimension on the global architectural stage, was also the final legacy of the brotherly cooperation between Piano and these two great engineers.

▶ While all energies in the Genoa office of the Building Workshop were focused on the Osaka Airport terminal, in Paris Renzo Piano and Bernard Plattner, a close associate since 1973, were drawing up the competition entry for a masterplan to reconstruct the Potsdamer Platz area of Berlin.[12] Whereas the Kansai terminal was the high point of a group method of working, the Potsdamer Platz project contained in embryo many of the urban development strategies that Piano and his colleagues were to explore more deeply in

THE ARTIFICIAL ISLAND,
4.37 x 1.25 KILOMETRES,
ON WHICH THE NEW
TERMINAL STANDS,
OUT IN OSAKA BAY.

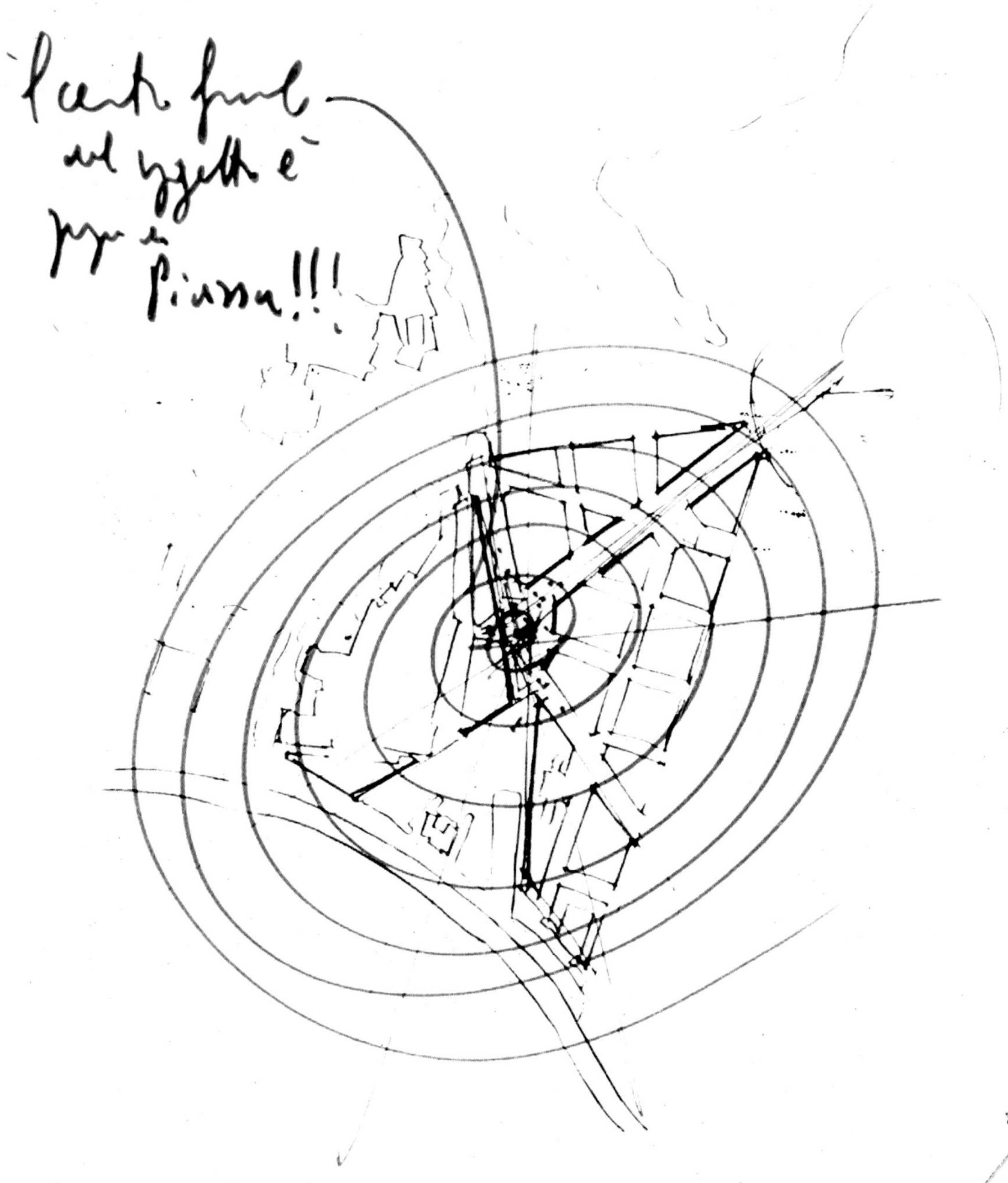

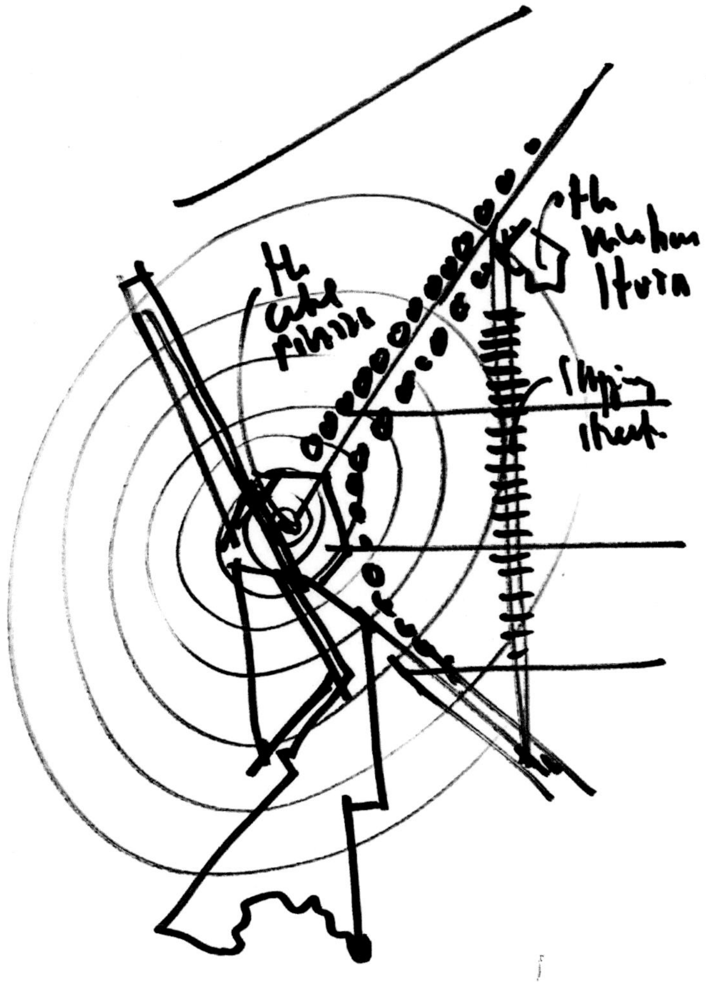

132

FROM RENZO PIANO'S FIRST
SKETCHES, THE CREATION OF
A NEW SQUARE WAS CLEARLY
THE DRIVING FORCE BEHIND
THE WHOLE OPERATION TO
RECONSTRUCT THE POTSDAMER
PLATZ AREA, 1992.

THE BACKBONE OF BUILDINGS
DESIGNED BY THE RPBW, WITH
THE COVERED ARKADE AREA ON THE
LEFT AND CULMINATING IN THE
DEBIS HEAD OFFICE FRONTING
THE LANDWEHRKANAL, 2000.

subsequent projects. And while the Kansai terminal project was the driving force in the expansion and consolidation of the Genoa office of the Building Workshop, the Potsdamer Platz development had a similar effect on the Paris office, which grew in the mid-1990s and moved to its present premises in the Rue des Archives.[13]

The fall of the Berlin Wall and the unification of Germany in 1989 triggered a series of projects for the new capital city and its nodal points. Potsdamer Platz, the epicentre of the city's golden age in the decades before the rise of Nazism, had been razed to the ground by bombing in World War II, and then divided by the infamous Wall after 1961.

In the 1980s Daimler-Benz had acquired a plot of land in the western part of the area, between the Wall and the Kulturforum, with a view to building a Berlin office for its service company Debis. After the fall of the Wall, a plot that had seemed dangerous and impossible to develop was bang in the centre of a hub area of the new Berlin. In 1992 Daimler-Benz, in conjunction with the municipality, launched an international competition, inviting selected tenderers to present a masterplan for the building of housing, offices and retail outlets on an area of 6.8 hectares delimited by the Potsdamer Platz metro station, the Staatsbibliothek, the Landwehrkanal and the plot Daimler-Benz had previously acquired.[14]

One of the strengths of the competition entry for the Kansai Airport terminal had been that it adopted in full the preliminary layout drawn up by Aéroport de Paris. Conversely, the factor that favoured the Building Workshop in winning the Berlin competition was the binning of an earlier development plan for the area that resurrected the traditional *mietkasernen* system – an orthogonal grid of compact blocks arranged around courtyards, which would have isolated both the Debis site and the new district from the Kulturforum and

the Tiergarten.[15] The planning and architectural solutions contained in the masterplan proposed by the Building Workshop were not intended to do the impossible, in other words to replicate the historical and typological heritage of the area, but to connect the *tabula rasa* of Potsdamer Platz to the living fabric of the city, and restore to the area the role of cultural and social epicentre it had enjoyed at the dawn of the 20th century.[16]

The main thrust of Renzo Piano's proposal was to foster culture. He planned for a number of cultural buildings not required by the programme, including a new theatre backing onto the rear of the Staatsbibliothek, which would integrate and connect the Potsdamer Platz area with the Kulturforum. This theatre is accessed from a new square, another feature not required by the competition specification. Named the Marlene Dietrich Platz, the square lies at the heart of the

network of streets connecting the district to the surrounding traffic arteries: the Alte Potsdamer Strasse, the only street surviving from the past, now remodelled as a tree-lined avenue connecting the square to the metro station; the Eichhornstrasse, which crosses the site from north to south; and other lesser streets dividing the residential blocks. Piano also proposed a triangular-shaped artificial lake, connected to the Landwehrkanal, which juts into the southern side of the area and borders the longer side of the Debis site.[17]

The creation of a new public space was the key aspect of the Building Workshop's proposal, not only by laying out squares, lakes and tree-lined avenues, but also within the residential blocks and individual buildings: the leafy courtyards of the blocks along the Alte Potsdamer Strasse; the Arkade, an impressive covered shopping centre on three levels that traverses the eastern part of the project area from north to south; and the imposing glazed-roof atrium of the Debis building, measuring 82 x 14 metres. In addition, the Building Workshop decreed that the ground floors of all buildings in the new district must be set back,

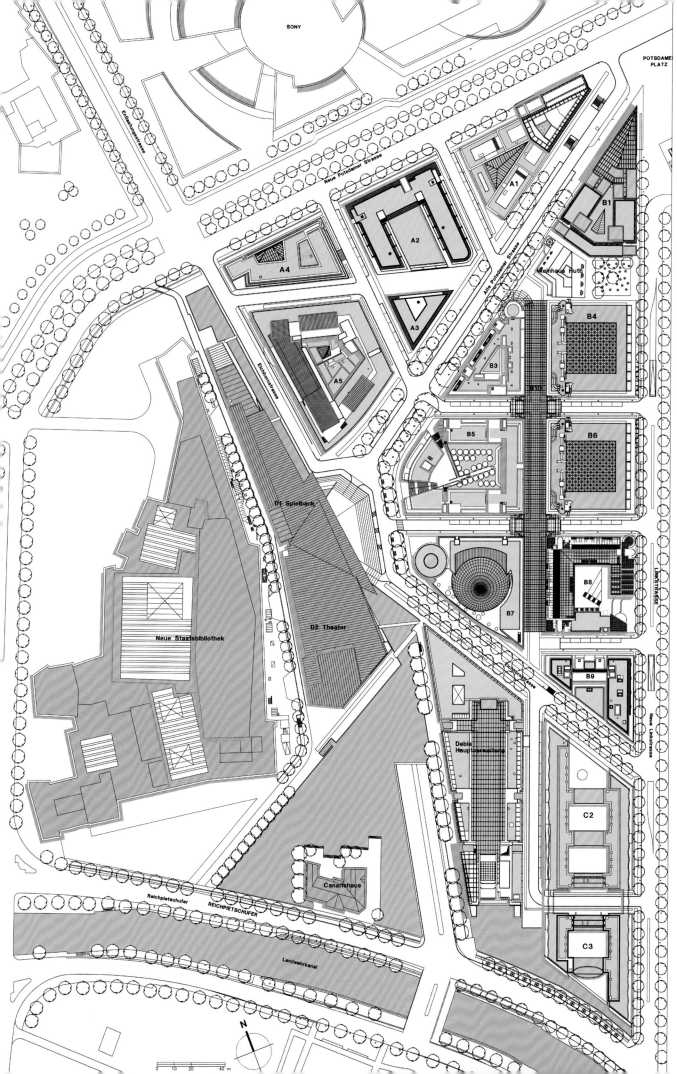

SONY

POTSDAME
PLATZ

Neue Potsdamer Strasse

Alte Potsdamer Strasse

Ertbaumstrasse

A1

B1

A2

A4

Weinhaus Huth

A3

B4

B3

A10

B5

B6

Eichhornstrasse

D1 Spielbank

B8

D2 Theater

B7

LINKSTRASSE

Neue Staatsbibliothek

Neue Linkstrasse

B9

Debis
Hauptverwaltung

Canarishaus

C2

Reichpietschufer REICHPIETSCHUFER

Landwehrkanal

C3

PLAN OF THE NEW BUILDINGS OF
THE POTSDAMER PLATZ DISTRICT,
BORDERED BY THE ARTIFICIAL
LAKE TO THE SOUTH, THE MARLENE
DIETRICH PLATZ IN THE CENTRE
AND THE TREE-LINED AVENUES
THAT CONVERGE ON IT.

N

0 10 20 30 40 m

making room for porticos and covered loggias at ground-floor level.

Victory in the 1992 competition allowed the Building Workshop to plan and design the public spaces of the new district and 50 per cent of the new buildings – a continuous backbone that starts from the Potsdamer Platz Banhof in the north-east, runs via the Arkade and the blocks to the west of it, and culminates in the Debis building. The Building Workshop was also responsible for the 'cultural pole' between the Staatsbibliothek and the Marlene Dietrich Platz, where the theatre and a casino are now sited. Piano and his colleagues also made further additions to the masterplan and were authorized to give instructions to the architects who designed the remainder of the buildings, regarding, for instance, the maximum height of the ground-floor parapets, loggias and porticos, and the use of terracotta for cladding purposes.[18]

In designing and constructing this series of buildings between 1993 and 2000 – and managing a massive project involving more than a hundred contractors and up to four thousand workers on

THE DEBIS HEADQUARTERS,
ON THE SOUTHERN EDGE OF
THE POTSDAMER PLATZ AREA,
FRONTS A NEW ARTIFICIAL LAKE.

138

VISITORS ACCESS THE
ENTRANCE AND FOYER
OF THE NEW THEATRE
FROM THE MARLENE
DIETRICH PLATZ, HEART
OF THE RPBW'S URBAN
DEVELOPMENT PLAN.

a daily basis, the Building Workshop continued to experiment with terracotta components for dry assembly. These had already featured in earlier projects: the Porto Antico (Old Harbour) in Genoa (1985–1992) and the residential buildings of the Cité Internationale in Lyon (1986–2006) and the Rue de Meaux in Paris (1987–1991). The ventilated facades are clad in terracotta components attached to metal armatures, with openings for windows, balconies and loggias. The terracotta components alternate with glazed facings and roofing, exposed or sheltered by awnings made of thin extrusions of terracotta – a technique later used for the New York Times building in Manhattan (2000–2007). At ground-floor level the buildings are supported on steel pillars, creating a visual and spatial connection between the public space of the streets and squares and the semi-public courtyards and entrance halls. In the Potsdamer Platz development, as in his urban planning projects of the 2000s, Piano showed no interest in recreating the past by replicating streets and buildings that no longer exist; rather he reconnected and gave new life to the urban fabric by introducing cultural buildings, creating public space and, as far as possible, opening up the ground floors of privately owned buildings to the city around them.[19] This was a strategy that we shall see repeated in the projects examined in the following chapter.

THE PUBLIC SPACE OF THE MARLENE
DIETRICH PLATZ SEEN FROM THE
COVERED ENTRANCE TO THE NEW
THEATRE. IN THE BACKGROUND, THE
RESIDENTIAL BUILDINGS DESIGNED
BY THE RPBW.

The successful completion of two complex, large-scale projects such as the Kansai Airport terminal and the reconstruction of the Potsdamer Platz area accelerated the growth of the Building Workshop, and inevitably led to change. Many of Piano's colleagues who had been with him since the 1970s or 1980s left the practice, and Shunji Ishida and Bernard Plattner became the key figures in the Genoa and Paris offices respectively. Moreover, many young architects who cut their teeth on the Osaka and Berlin projects are now Building Workshop Partners, for example Emanuela Baglietto, Giorgio Bianchi, Antoine Chaaya and Joost Moolhuijzen.[20]

However, this ongoing dynamic of growth was in danger of compromising the quality of the practice's planning and technological research. Renzo Piano therefore decided on a structure capable of rising to the challenge of large-scale projects, and he organized operations with a clear division of labour and internal hierarchy. But he restricted the number of staff and offices so that he could follow all projects personally.

In 1997, on Renzo Piano's sixtieth birthday, the managerial and organizational structure of the Building Workshop was established by allocating shareholdings to Piano himself and a number of Partners and associates. This regulated and crystalized a hierarchical pyramid that in fact already existed, with a number of project leaders, now Partners, working with Piano on the planning and management of the practice's projects and offices. Since the late 1990s, despite its ever-growing international reputation, the Renzo Piano Building Workshop has relied on around 150 co-workers – architects, modellers, IT operatives and BIM managers, archivists, legal experts, administrators and so on, almost all of whom are employed in the Genoa or Paris offices, in the cities where Piano has lived and worked since 1971.[21]

In the 1990s Piano opted for a compromise between two extremes: strictly personal and authorial project management, on the one hand; and the inevitably detached management of a large global partnership, on the other – between Glenn Murcutt and Foster + Partners, to mention two examples at opposite ends of the project management spectrum. He has organized a practice that is constantly straining to maintain a balance between his personal authority and the creative freedom of a cohesive group of co-workers.[22]

[1] See Marc Bédarida, 'Cultiver le sensible', in *Renzo Piano, un regard construit*, Éditions du Centre Pompidou, Paris 2000, pp. 32–42.

[2] Reflecting on the Berlin project, Renzo Piano commented: 'This is by far the most difficult job we have done', in Renzo Piano, *The Poetics of Construction*, School of Architecture and Planning, Massachusetts Institute of Technology, Cambridge (MA) 2002, p. 65.

[3] See *The Making of Kansai International Airport*, Kodansha, Tokyo 1004; 'Kansai International Airport Passenger Terminal Building' monographic issue of *Japan Architect*, 15, 1994; 'Kansai' in *The Architectural Review*, 1173, 1994; Peter Buchanan, *Renzo Piano Building Workshop. Complete Works, III*, Phaidon, London 1997, pp. 128–227.

[4] The decision to locate the new terminal in the sea and away from the urban area meant that the airport could be operational 24/7. A two-level bridge 3.75 km in length connects the island to the mainland; the upper level carries a main road, the lower two railway lines.

[5] Paul Andreu, 'The Concept of the Kansai International Airport Terminal', in *Kansai International Airport Passenger Terminal Building*, op. cit., pp. 18–19; Philip Jodidio, *Paul Andreu Architect*, Birkhäuser, Basel 2004, pp. 104–107.

[6] A factor in the invitation issued to the RPBW was probably the fact that two of Piano's closest collaborators – Noriaki Okabe and Shunji Ishida – were Japanese, and that the Paris office of his practice had already worked with Aéroport de Paris on a joint project for Expo '89. See also *The Making of Kansai International Airport*, op. cit., pp. 64–70.

[7] Piano's acceptance of the Aéroport de Paris layout, rather than imposing a new vision of his own, was a decisive factor in the award of the contract to the RPBW.

[8] See *The Making of Kansai International Airport*, op. cit., pp. 90–95; Alistair Guthrie, 'Engineering Innovation', in *Renzo Piano. The Art of Making Buildings*, Royal Academy of Arts, London 2018, pp. 133–134.

[9] The studies for integrating the various services into the structure and roofing of the terminal were carried out by Tom Barker and Alistair Guthrie, engineers with Ove Arup & Partners. See Philip Dilley, Alistair Guthrie, 'Kansai International Airport Terminal Building', in *Arup Journal*, 1, 1995, pp. 14–23.

[10] For a discussion of how construction and information technology is used by the Building Workshop, see the recent work by Sergio Russo Ermolli and Giuliano Galluccio, *Materia, Prodotto, Dato. Il valore dell'informazione nelle architetture del Renzo Piano Building Workshop*, Maggioli, Sant'Arcangelo di Romagna 2021. See also Renzo Piano, *La responsabilità dell'architetto*, Passigli, Florence 2004, pp. 25–29.

[11] The project documentation was all sent, and is now kept, at the Renzo Piano Foundation, Projects Archive, RPBW Collection, Kansai International Airport Passenger Terminal Building 1988–1994.

[12] See Peter Buchanan, *Renzo Piano Building Workshop. Complete Works, IV*, Phaidon, London 2000, pp. 156–213.

[13] Fulvio Irace, 'In Bottega', in *Renzo Piano. The Art of Making Buildings*, Royal Academy of Arts, London 2018, p. 103.

[14] Daimler-Benz already had positive experience of the RPBW, which was planning the Mercedes Benz Design Centre in Sindelfingen.

[15] The architects Heinz Hilmer and Christoph Sattler had won an earlier competition to develop the area between the Potsdamer Platz and the Leipziger Platz, following the instructions of City Architect Hans Stimman. However, this plan did not come to fruition. See Christoph Sattler, 'Potsdamer Platz – Leipziger Platz, Berlin 1991', in *The Architectural Design*, 1–2, 1993, pp. 18–23. A review of the competition entries is published in Peter Rumpf, 'La città dei concorsi: Berlino del "dopo muro"', in *Rassegna*, 61, 1995, pp. 44–50.

[16] A programme set forth in the speech that Piano gave in Berlin on the day of the inauguration of the new Potzdamer Platz, reported in *Renzo Piano 2004*, op. cit., pp. 93–99.

[17] Renzo Piano, 'Il mestiere più antico del mondo', in *Micromega*, 2, 1996, pp. 109–110.

[18] Richard Rogers, Lauber & Wöhr and Arata Isozaki designed the blocks along the Linkstrasse, Rafael Moneo a new hotel on the Marlene Dietrich Platz, and Hans Kollhoff the triangular building between the Potsdamer Strasse and the Alte Potsdamer Strasse. For the wealth of documentation drawn up by the Building Workshop, see Renzo Piano Foundation, Projects Archive, RPBW Collection, Potsdamer Platz 1992–2000.

[19] Claudia Conforti, 'Levigate artificiosità', in *Casabella*, 656, 1998, pp. 62–63, 74–81.

[20] Conversation between the author and Emanuela Baglietto, Genoa, 25 May 2021, and with Antoine Chaaya, Genoa, 22 October 2021.

[21] During the years of the Kansai Airport terminal project, the Building Workshop opened an office in Osaka, while from 2007 to 2019 they had an active office in New York. However, neither of these offices ever had the number of staff or importance of the permanent offices in Genoa and Paris. They functioned more as outposts in particularly promising markets.

[22] According to Kenneth Frampton: 'In no architectural practice today is the contribution of colleagues so openly acknowledged as at the Renzo Piano Building Workshop.' See Kenneth Frampton, preface to Renzo Piano, *Giornale di bordo*, Passigli, Florence 1997, p. 7.

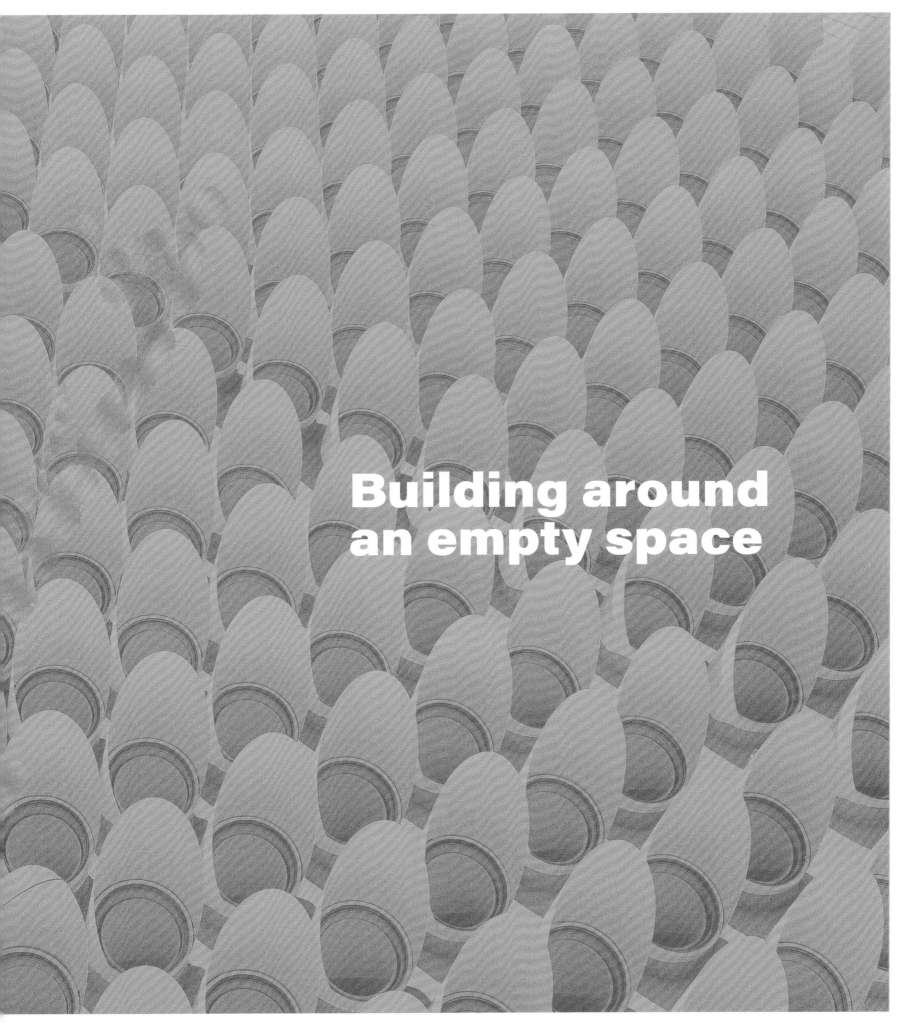

Building around an empty space

Although Renzo Piano's formation and instincts as an architect were born of a love of experimentation in construction and technical/technological research, over time his attention was drawn increasingly to urban settings and the shaping of public space, following his vital experiences with the Pompidou Centre, the District Workshops (*Laboratori di Quartiere*) and the reconstruction of the Potsdamer Platz area. With these Piano had had to come to terms with the history and urban dynamics of two of Europe's major cities, as well as those of smaller historic centres.[1]

While Italian design culture in the second half of the 20th century made its mark on the international scene by exploring the connections between political militancy, historical/urban analysis and planning interventions – think for a moment of such figures as Aldo Rossi, Carlo Aymonino, Paolo Portoghesi or Vittorio Gregotti perhaps – Piano adopted a very different way of doing things. His approach to established urban settings is totally non-ideological and non-theoretical but rather intuitive, experiential and above all project-based, making him a very rare bird among the Italian architects of his generation. Significantly, he has written nothing on the history or theory of architecture.[2] The happy 'contamination' between city and architecture, the private dimension and the public space is played out within the limits of the particular project, in each case determined by the principal characteristics of the location and the specification dictated by the client. A project is not an opportunity to try out premeditated theories or models; on the contrary, it has been through Piano's accumulation of practical experiences and the projects he has managed – what he calls the *cultura di fare* (hands-on culture) – that he has arrived at certain compositional strategies.[3] In the following pages we shall see the further development of this approach, focusing on the restoration of Genoa's Porto Antico (Old Harbour) (1985–2001) and extensions to the High Museum of

Art in Atlanta (1999–2005) and the Morgan Library in New York (2000–2006). These projects demonstrate how, for Piano, the careful design of empty space – squares of all shapes and sizes, entrance ways, walkways and so on – is just as important as the modelling of the buildings around them. Moreover, it is often the insertion and formation of such open spaces, in many cases not required by the specification, that inspire a project and give it life, as, for example, with the Marlene Dietrich Platz in his reconstruction of the Potsdamer Platz area. The square – 'the idea of open space as a place of meeting and conviviality, the idea of living life in square and street' – is for Piano the key aspect of European urban culture, and the link that joins the past, or 'tradition', with the future of the cities in which he has been invited to work.[4]

▶ Since 1981 Renzo Piano has been much involved with his home city of Genoa, in particular its harbour frontage, from east to west, and he still has several studies on the go.[5] The restoration of the Porto Antico (1985–2001) is maybe the most significant and enduring urban project so far undertaken by Piano and his colleagues. It is a paradigm of his ability to work in the gaps, to lend dignity to waste places, to reconnect dilapidated fragments to the consolidated fabric of the city.[6] This was also the project that led to the founding of the Genoa office – before the scaling-up triggered by the Kansai International Airport terminal. Some of the colleagues in the former Atelier Piano & Rice worked there, for instance Shunji Ishida and Venanzio Truffelli, as well as many of the young architects who in the following decades became first associates then Partners of the Italian branch of the Building Workshop: Mark Carroll, Donald Hart, Emanuela Baglietto, Giorgio Bianchi, Giorgio Grandi and Olaf De Nooyer.[7]

As in all cities that owe their wealth to the sea, Genoa's harbour has always been its beating heart: from the first wooden jetties projecting from its ancient districts to the massive warehouses and other infrastructure that accompanied its industrial growth in the 19th and 20th centuries.[8] In use until the post-war years – Piano himself often mentions how as a child he would go with his father to watch the merchant ships being loaded and unloaded,[9] the Porto Antico was gradually abandoned in the 1960s with the opening of the Porto Nuovo (New Harbour), and then the industrial and commercial facilities at Cornigliano and Prà shifted Genoa's industrial development to the western outskirts.[10]

By the 1980s, the Porto Antico area, close to the historic city centre, the Cathedral of San Lorenzo, the Castello district, the Sottoripa arcades and the Palazzo San Giorgio, was in a state of decay and inaccessible to the people of Genoa, obstructed by the elevated expressway – the intrusive relief road built between 1961 and 1965 – and the gates blocking access to the sea.[11]

The first plans for the Porto Antico date back to 1981, when the municipal authority asked Renzo Piano to apply his District Workshop method to the Molo area. Although this initiative went no further than the

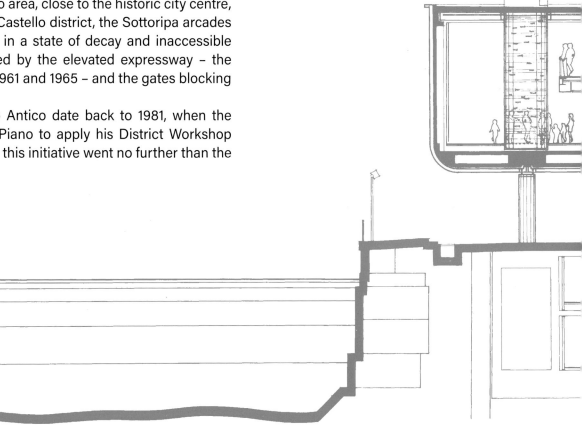

CROSS-SECTION OF THE HUGE
TANKS OF GENOA'S AQUARIUM ON
THE PONTE SPINOLA, CREATED AND
OPENED FOR EXPO COLOMBIANA
IN 1992.

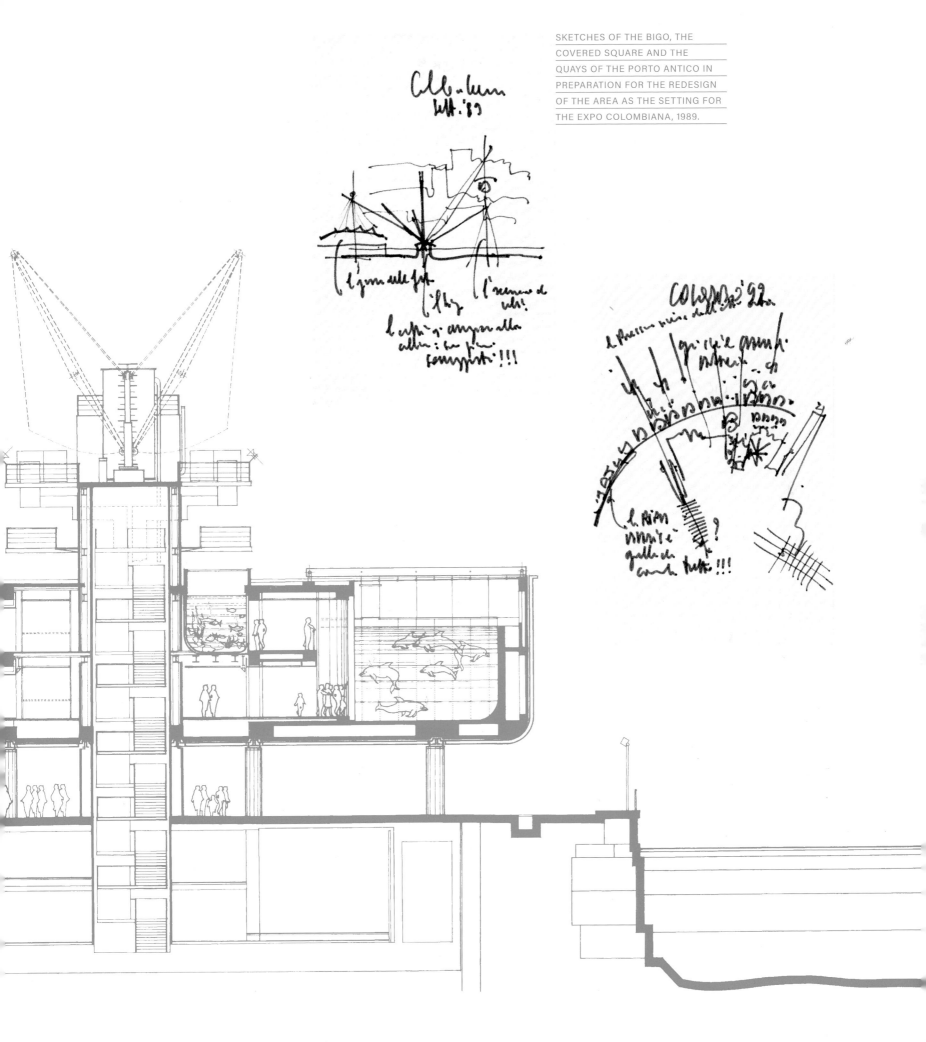

SKETCHES OF THE BIGO, THE COVERED SQUARE AND THE QUAYS OF THE PORTO ANTICO IN PREPARATION FOR THE REDESIGN OF THE AREA AS THE SETTING FOR THE EXPO COLOMBIANA, 1989.

BUILDING AROUND AN EMPTY SPACE   149

GENOA'S PORTO ANTICO
FOLLOWING ITS
RECONFIGURATION AND
OPENING FOR THE 1992
EXPOSITION.

planning stage, his studies for the residential blocks, the *carrugi* (narrow lanes) and their relationship with the sea made Piano aware of the potential this neglected area could have for the city of Genoa.[12] In 1984 the municipal authority again asked the Building Workshop to propose a project for Expo 1992, marking the 500th anniversary of the European colonization of America. In agreement with the municipal administration, Piano decided that, rather than design a series of pavilions on a peripheral site, he would restore the entire Porto Antico area, enriching it with new public and private functions and reconnecting it with the living fabric of the city in a way that would outlast the short period of Expo 1992.[13]

The intervention strategy adopted by Piano and his colleagues was based on the central importance of maintaining fluidity of movement inside and outside of buildings, whose walls were to serve as 'screens' projecting a sense of the area's history and identity. There were two aspects to the project: an immaterial aspect – the public space, continuous and indivisible, charged with meaning, uniting the public areas to those enclosed and separate within the buildings; and the concrete aspect, heavy and geometrically defined, of the external walls of the various buildings sited there.[14] For Piano, facades representing the old tradition of building embody a heritage of values shared by the city and its people, often regardless of their objective architectural worth.[15] This principle was behind the decision to preserve the large factory buildings of the Porto Antico, simply because the economic prosperity and social cohesion of the city's community had been founded on them, even though they had long been abandoned and were not necessarily of great architectural or constructional merit.

Removing the gates and routing a section of the relief road underground below the flyover created a new public space: the Piazza Caricamento. This 'liberated' the Palazzo San Giorgio, reconnected the arcaded streets of Sottoripa with the sea and made it possible to pedestrianize the route that leads from Piazza Ferrari down the Via San Lorenzo to the Cathedral and on to the historic harbour quays. In the area between Palazzo San Giorgio and the sea, work was done to restore the 17th-century Customs Warehouses and convert the imposing Millo building into retail

THE TENSILE STRUCTURES OF THE BIGO AND THE PIAZZA DELLE FESTE, EMBLEMATIC OF THE RPBW'S INTERVENTION FOR EXPO '92, ARE STILL SYMBOLS OF THE RECONNECTION OF THE PORTO ANTICO TO THE CITY OF GENOA.

outlets and hospitality venues, demolishing only certain parts of the upper storeys to soften their stereometry. Opposite were constructed the Bigo and the completely new Piazza delle Feste – an open-sided flexible space for putting on shows and plays, which has a steel tensile-structure roof featuring Teflon 'sails'. Symbol of Expo 1992, the Bigo is a structure consisting of hollow steel arms, bolted to a water-level base plate and held in tension by steel cables supporting a panoramic lift. To the right of the Bigo, on the Ponte Spinola and the new Via del Mare, were cast the reinforced-concrete columns supporting the linear sequence of huge exposed tanks that make up the Aquarium, to which were added in 2001 the Biosphere and in 2013 the Cetaceans Pavilion.[16] Along the Calata Molo Vecchio to the left tower the imposing Cotton Warehouses, built in the early 20th century by British engineers and enlarged in the following decades. Here again, rather than impose his own ideas, Piano stuck strictly to his principles of

respect: the facades were saved and restored, as were the interiors of the original nucleus, graced with attractive cast-iron columns, whereas the more recent buildings were entirely gutted. During Expo '92, they housed the pavilions of the participating nations and subsequently a conference centre, a cinema, a library and commercial premises and restaurants.[17] To one side, a similar parallelepiped-shaped building with a metal structure and facade of prefabricated terracotta components contains the technical installations, offices, service areas and a huge multistorey car park serving the Porto Antico area.

The Building Workshop's intervention consisted of a balanced programme of demolitions,

restorations, conversions and new buildings. Notwithstanding the quality and fortunes of the individual operations – especially the Aquarium, which soon became one of the city's and the region's greatest attractions, Piano's intervention is distinguished by an absence of ego-tripping and 'spectacular' buildings, which, in fact, take a back seat. The real driver of the operation was the public space, with its calibrated design and precise hierarchy: from the open space of Piazza Caricamento to the palm-shaded walkway of the Calata Cattaneo, set off by the spars of Japanese sculptor Sumusu Shingu's Bigo; from the shady arcades of Sottoripa to the blazing marine light of the Isola delle Chiatte at the far end of the Ponte Spinola.[18]

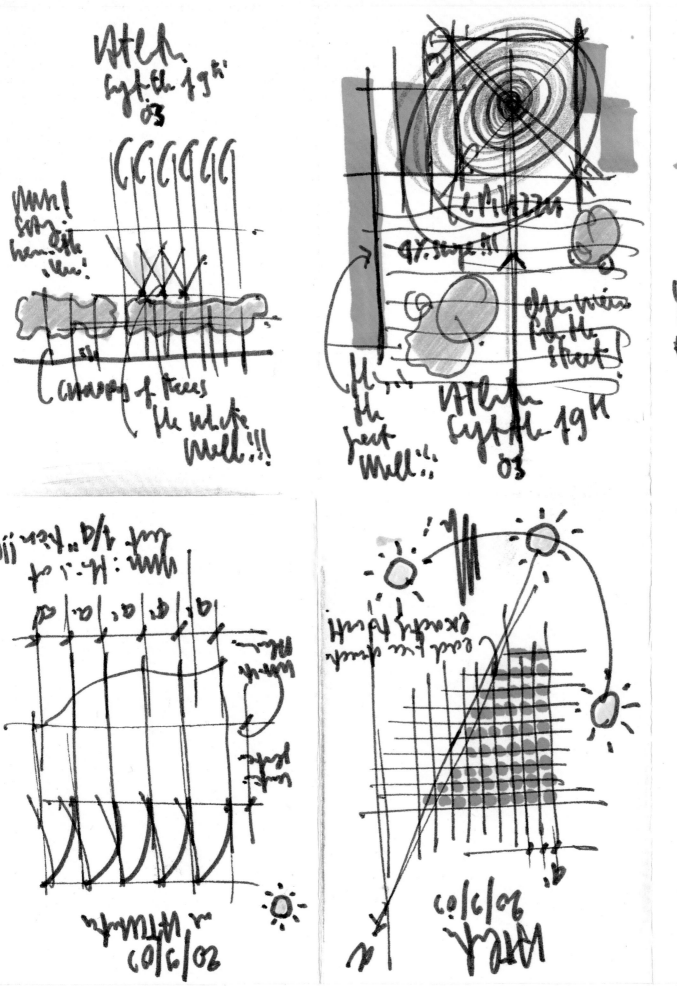
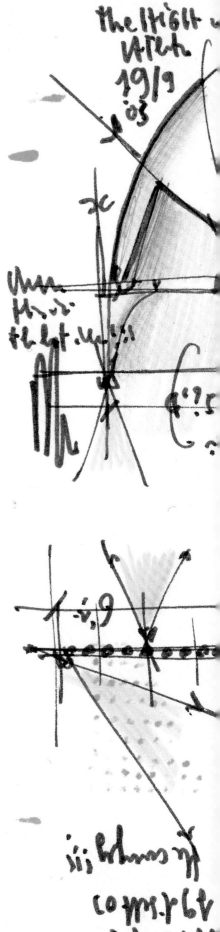

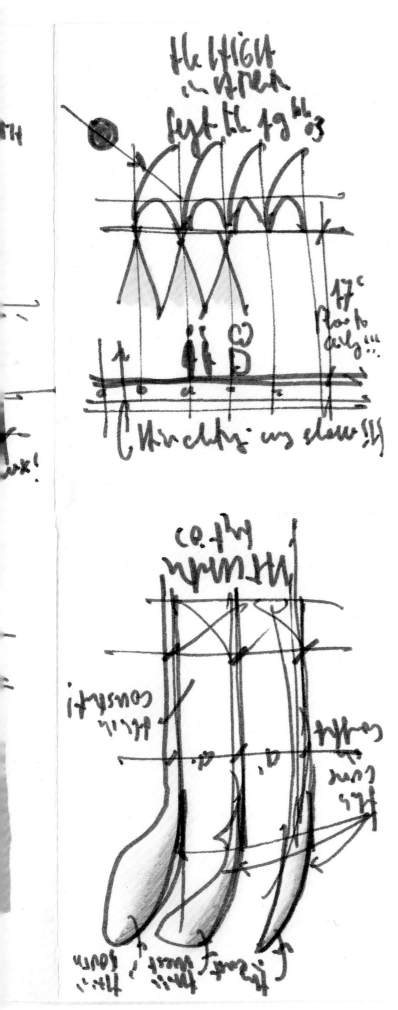

► Piano's proven ability to fulfil clients' requirements effectively, while being able to interpret and 'bend' a project specification to create public space in the service of established urban environments, is maybe the principal reason for the resounding success enjoyed by the Building Workshop in the United States over the last twenty years. With the architectural excesses of the so-called Postmodern and Deconstructivist movements consigned to oblivion, the calculated elegance of the Menil Collection – and its delicate insertion in a traditional residential suburb, as if it had always been present – became the benchmark for many American clients and museum curators. Certainly they entrusted a surprising number of commissions to the RPBW: from the Nasher Sculpture Center in Dallas (1999–2003) to the California Academy of Sciences in San Francisco (2000–2008), from the extension to the Art Institute of Chicago (2000–2009) to those for the LACMA in Los Angeles (2003–2010), the Isabella Stewart Gardner Museum in Boston (2005–2012), the Harvard Art Museum (2006–2014) and the Kimbell Museum in Fort Worth (2007–2013) and, more recently, the new premises for the Whitney Museum of American Art in Manhattan (2007–2015), to mention just a few of the projects the practice has successfully completed in the United States.[19]

The fact that many of these are extensions cannot be a coincidence. Clients have recognized his talent for working with pre-existing structures, enlarging and enhancing them without disruption or egocentric

RENZO PIANO IS IN THE HABIT OF FOLDING AN A4 SHEET INTO EIGHT TO MAKE SKETCHES OF A FUTURE BUILDING: THIS MEANS HE ALWAYS RETAINS AN OVERALL VISION OF THE IDEAS HE IS PURSUING.

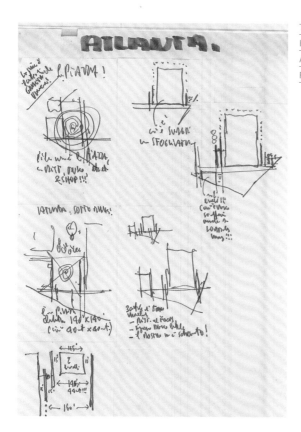

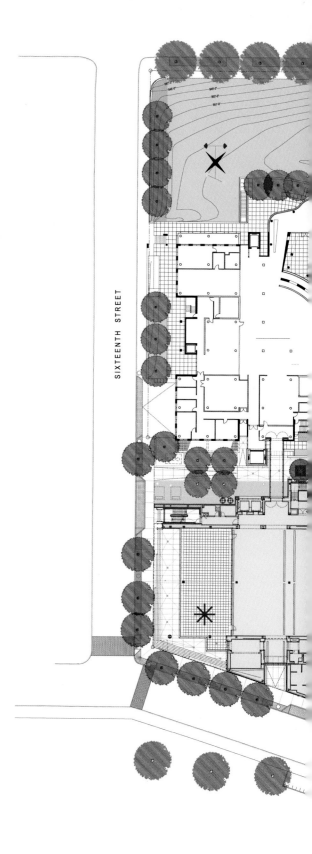

SIXTEENTH STREET

gestures, and at the same time reconnecting them to their urban setting by arranging them around empty spaces designed as new places of meeting and city life. This talent was demonstrated by two seminal works, both planned in the early 2000s: his extensions to the High Museum of Art in Atlanta (1999–2005) and the Morgan Library in New York (2000–2006).

Founded in 1905, Atlanta's High Museum of Art is one of America's most important cultural centres. In the 1990s the continuing acquisition of works of art, and the need for flexible spaces to accommodate the large sculptures and installations typical of contemporary creativity, made it necessary to enlarge the 'historic' building designed by Richard Meier & Partners between 1979 and 1983. As well as doubling the exhibition space, the Board asked Piano to plan new areas for workshops and administrative offices.[20]

During his first visit to Atlanta in 1998, Piano soon realized that the High Museum was very close to another cultural centre of importance for the city: the Woodruff Arts Center, which included the premises of the Atlanta Symphony Orchestra, the Alliance Theatre and the College of Art. Squeezed between a busy highway and the residential suburb of Winn Park, this citadel of the arts was located in a block on the northern edge of Midtown, in a setting without city-centre facilities or shared meeting areas.

Given these considerations, Piano agreed with Michael Shapiro, then director of the High Museum, that he should first draw up a masterplan for the area, before

IT IS EVIDENT FROM THE GROUND
PLAN OF THE BLOCK THAT THE NEW
BUILDINGS OF THE HIGH MUSEUM WERE
DESIGNED WITH URBAN PLANNING IN
MIND: TO CREATE A NEW SQUARE AND
TO COMPLETE THE STREET FRONTAGES.

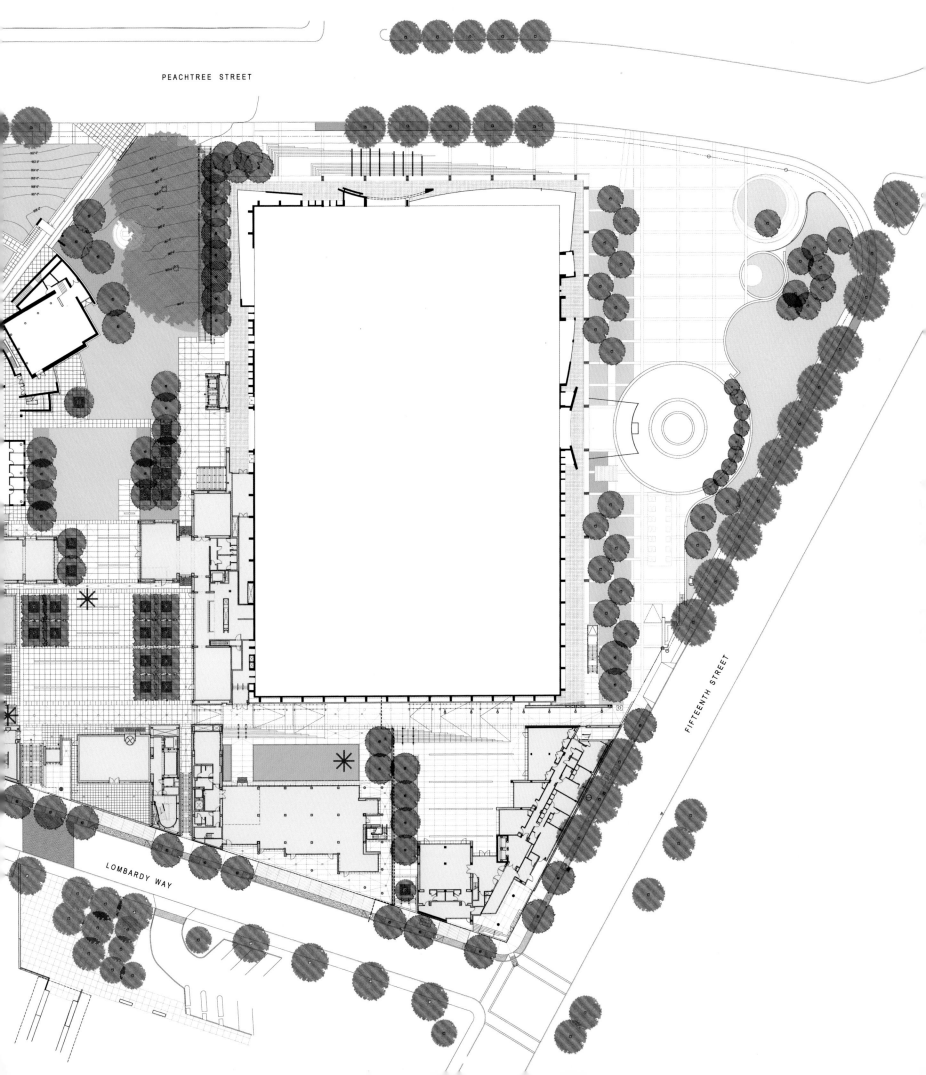

PEACHTREE STREET

LOMBARDY WAY

FIFTEENTH STREET

designing the museum extension. The idea was to create a 'campus' on which the museum buildings and those of the Woodruff Arts Center would be arranged around a new public square serving the district and the city as a whole.[21]

Choosing not to concentrate on a single building, but instead bringing a number of structures together, more in keeping with the scale of the city, and all around an empty space is a typical Piano strategy – consider, for example, his Parco della Musica Auditorium in Rome (1994–2002) – and it was certainly appropriate for the Atlanta project.[22] To fit in with the ground plan and height of the existing building designed by Richard Meier, the enlargement planned by the Building Workshop was broken down into three structures: the Wieland Pavilion, the Anne Cox Chambers Wing and an office building. These were set around a new pedestrianized square (paved in keeping with the various entry points and with a garden on the Peach Street side), which was connected to the neighbouring streets by flights of steps and other access ways.

The Wieland Pavilion, now incorporating the entrance to the High Museum, is the largest building, with galleries for the permanent collection and

THE ROOFING OF THE NEW PAVILIONS IS A CARPET OF CONICAL SKYLIGHTS WHICH, THANKS TO THEIR SHAPE AND ORIENTATION, ADMIT ONLY LIGHT FROM THE NORTH.

a generous amount of flexible space for temporary exhibitions. It is connected to Meier's building by a glazed overhead walkway and features an extensive panoramic terrace on which stands Claes Oldenburg and Coosje van Bruggen's *Balzac Pétanque* sculpture.[23] The Anne Cox Chambers Wing, smaller in size, is used for temporary exhibitions and stands beside the office building, which was designed to allow for a doubling of its internal space.

As with the Menil Collection, the cladding of the new buildings replicates and interprets the pre-existing finishings. The three buildings designed by the Building Workshop are linked together by their uniform cladding of vertically arranged and white-painted aluminium strips with an opaque finish, the closely configured pattern of which also ensures that the new additions fit in with the orthogonal cladding of the Meier building. On the ground floor, as usual with Piano, the transparent glass panels seem to lift the buildings off the ground, blurring the boundary between the public space of the square and the semi-private space of the museum lobby. The bookshop, restaurants and a bar are strategically located on the ground floor of the additions to lend animation to the square.

For Piano, the careful design of empty space – squares of all shapes and sizes, entrance ways, walkways and so on – is just as important as the modelling of the buildings around them.

The intense sunlight of Atlanta causes the new buildings of the High Museum of Art to shine and has also been a factor in the design of the roof structures – always a crucial element in Building Workshop projects. The Wieland Pavilion and the Anne Cox Chambers Wing are roofed with a thousand or so conical skylights surmounted by funnel-shaped components. These were carefully designed using models and mock-ups so as to capture the natural light from the north and channel it into the exhibition galleries below, gently illuminating the works of art on display.[24]

Kenneth Frampton describes the common factor in many of Renzo Piano's best works as 'a fleeting dimension of banality.'[25] Far from this being a negative judgement, he sees this banality as the 'highest possible achievement of an architect' who refuses the seductive temptation to impose his personal imprint, but chooses to harmonize the buildings he designs with the pre-existing scale, materials and stereometry of the location concerned.[26] Painstaking attention to detail, the use of natural

THE NEW SQUARE CONNECTS THE
ORIGINAL HIGH MUSEUM BUILDING
DESIGNED BY RICHARD MEIER WITH
THE NEW ADDITIONS PLANNED BY
THE RPBW.

THE GLAZED FRONTAGES OF THE ATRIUM AND GROUND-FLOOR AREAS APPEAR TO RAISE THE BUILDINGS ABOVE THE PAVED APPROACHES AND CONNECT THE PUBLIC SPACE WITH THE INTERIOR OF THE MUSEUM.

HIGH MUSEUM OF ART

light precisely calibrated by layered roofing, and the connective tissue of public space are the areas in which the 'personal' contribution of Piano and his colleagues is most evident. The extension to the Morgan Library, begun in the same years as the High Museum of Art project, is further testimony to this approach.

► Founded in 1906 by John Pierpont Morgan, banker and omnivorous collector of both works of art and old books and manuscripts, the Morgan Library has over time come to occupy three buildings located around a compact block between Madison Avenue and Park Avenue in Manhattan: Morgan House, a building designed by Charles McKim, and a neo-Palladian annexe completed in 1928.[28] The ongoing growth of the collections, the need for more space and the ever-stricter accessibility and security standards required of museums led the institution to ask the Renzo Piano Building Workshop to undertake an organic project to enlarge and rationalize their premises. The three

THE GALLERIES OF THE HIGH
MUSEUM ARE CHARACTERIZED
BY RATIONAL USE OF SPACE AND
THE GENTLE NATURAL LIGHT
TYPICAL OF EXHIBITION VENUES
DESIGNED BY THE RPBW.

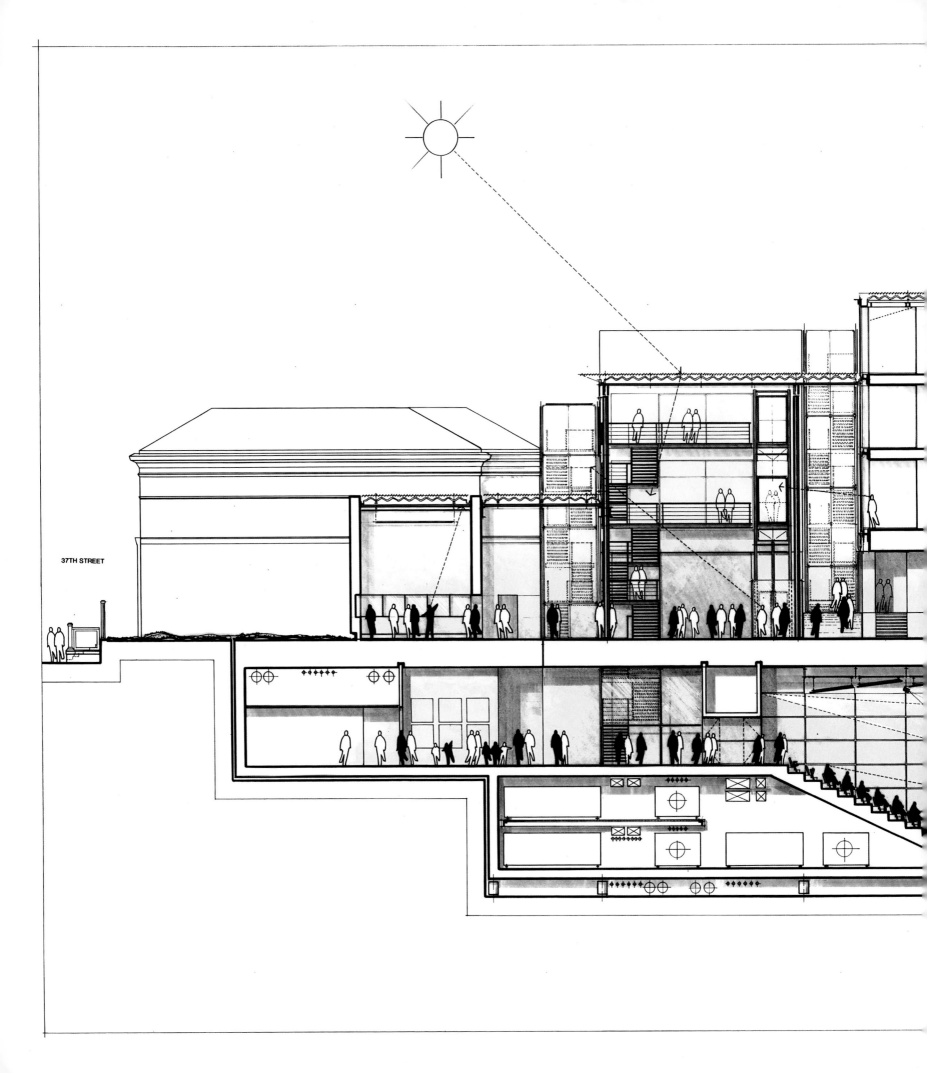

37TH STREET

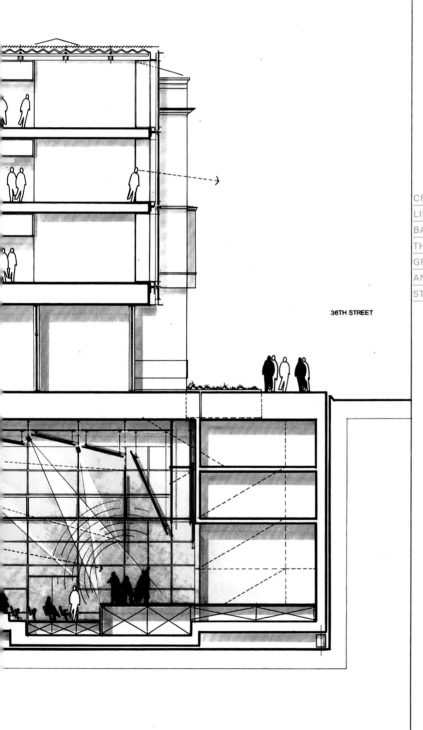

36TH STREET

CROSS-SECTION OF THE MORGAN
LIBRARY: THE EXCAVATION OF THE
BASEMENT AREA ENSURED THAT
THE NEW BUILDINGS VISIBLE ABOVE
GROUND RESPECTED THE VOLUMES
AND HEIGHTS OF THE PRE-EXISTING
STRUCTURES.

pre-existing buildings, classified as historic monuments in the changing cityscape of Manhattan, were to be carefully preserved. At the same time, they wanted to add a reading room, a three-hundred-seat auditorium, new galleries and storage facilities for the conservation of fragile manuscripts and works of art. Roughly 10,000 metres square of new space had to be accommodated in the oblong area between the existing buildings, without exceeding the rigid limits set for New York blocks.[28]

Instead of building upwards, creating a multistorey structure that would have crushed and diminished the presence of the historic buildings, Piano again chose the way of discretion: he would create the space for the auditorium,

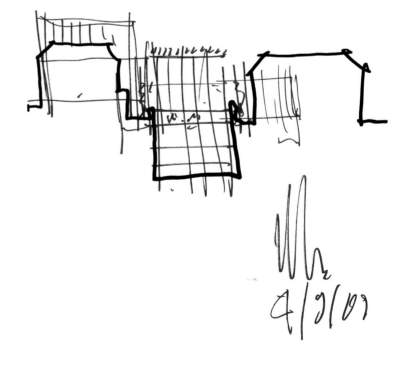

THE NEW PAVILIONS OF THE
MORGAN LIBRARY EFFECTIVELY
OCCUPY THE SPACES BETWEEN
PRE-EXISTING BUILDINGS,
THEIR DIFFERENT FUNCTIONS
CONNECTED BY A COURTYARD.

EXCAVATING THE HUGE BASEMENT
AREA, THE FIRST OPERATION TO
CREATE MORE SPACE FOR THE
MORGAN LIBRARY.

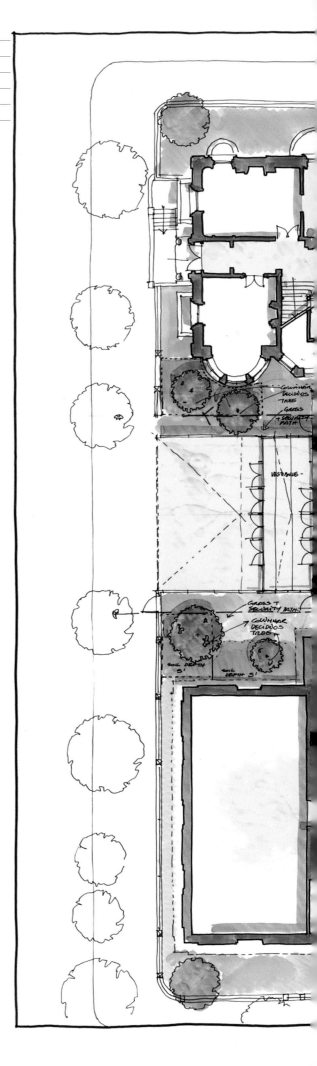

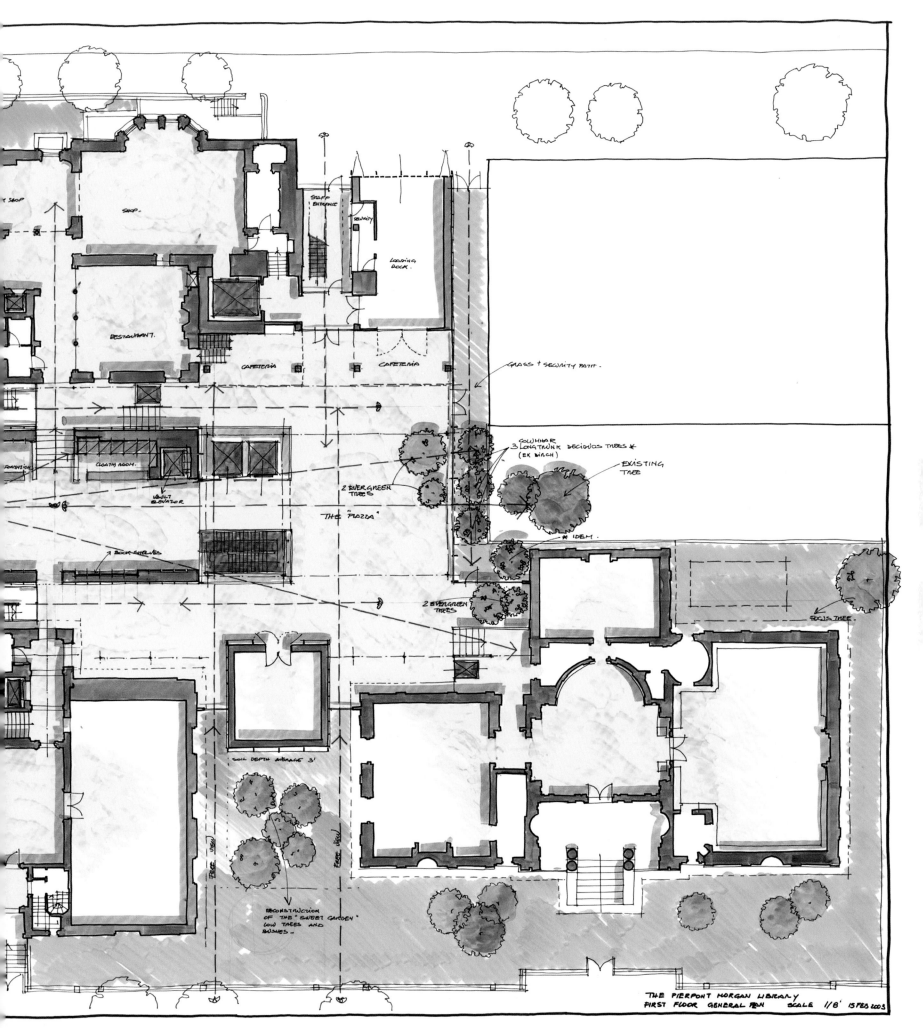

THE PIERPONT MORGAN LIBRARY
FIRST FLOOR GENERAL PLAN   SCALE 1/8"   15 FEB 2003

Piano has a predilection for working on the margins, in the gaps, on a small and medium scale, and proposing the minimum intervention required to enhance the public utility of a place.

the storerooms and the study and research facilities by digging down 17 metres into the earth. On the ground floor he located three pavilions, slotted in among the pre-existing buildings: on the Madison Avenue side the entrance and foyer, with an exhibition area on the first floor and a reading room on the second; on East 37th Street a three-storey building housing offices and service facilities; and on East 36th Street a small cubic structure, completely opaque, exclusively for exhibiting books and manuscripts. In the centre, at the heart of the whole operation, is a beautifully proportioned, entirely glass-enclosed public courtyard. This houses the intersection of all paths connecting the new annexes to the historic buildings.

A further sign of Piano's discretion: the frontages of the three additions stand back from the facade of Morgan House and the two early-20th-century buildings, while the light marble facings of the latter were the inspiration for the opaque white finish of the steel panels used for the uniform cladding of the Building Workshop structures. Steel alternates with glass to create a subtle rhythm of solids

THE NEW COURTYARD IS NOT ONLY A PLACE TO PAUSE AND MEET PEOPLE, BUT ALSO THE STARTING POINT OF THE ITINERARIES THAT CONNECT THE DIFFERENT PAVILIONS AND THE MANY FUNCTIONS OF THE LIBRARY.

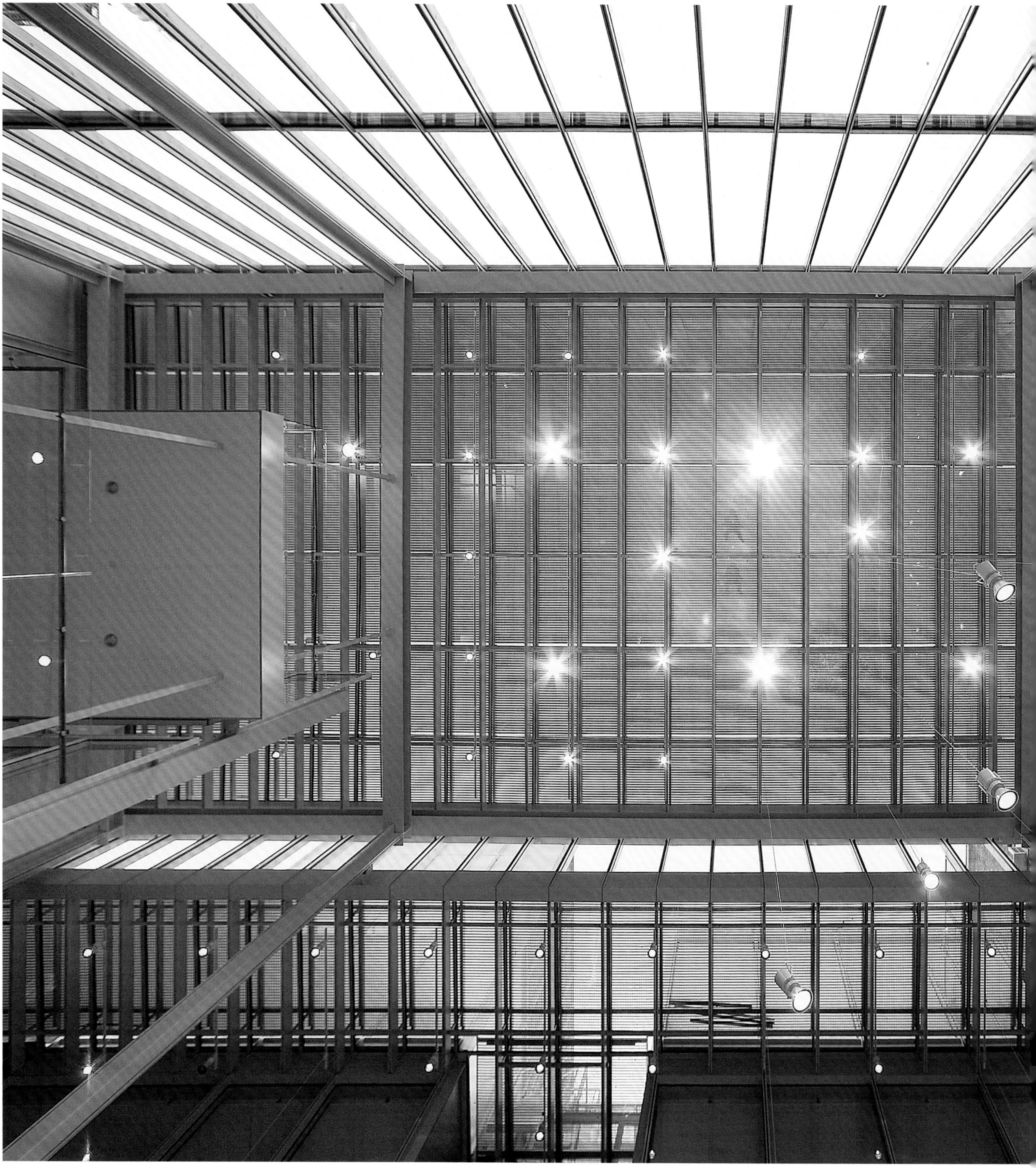

and voids across the new elevations,[29] for example the upper two thirds of the tripartite main elevation on Madison Avenue are opaque, while the bottom third consists entirely of glass. The gaze of passers-by and visitors is thus drawn from the street to the heart of the complex: the public courtyard. For the visitor, the compression of the entrance, obtained by reducing it in height and cladding it uniformly with wooden panels, is like a prelude to the three-times higher courtyard and the intense light that fills it.[30] Divided up by steel uprights and cross-members at different heights, all painted white, this space is encroached on by a protrusion of the office building and a walkway coming from the gallery above the atrium. Sitting at one of the tables in the centre of the courtyard before proceeding to the study rooms or exhibition spaces, the observant visitor can fully appreciate Renzo Piano's disciplined discretion and sensitivity to the spirit of place.[31]

THE DELICATE METAL FRAMEWORK
AND GLASS WALLS TRANSMUTE THE
COURTYARD AT THE HEART OF THE
MORGAN LIBRARY INTO A SHOWCASE
FILLED WITH NATURAL LIGHT.

[1] 'I have moved on from there... Making has now become part of a much bigger vision in our work, that now includes as equally important such things as history and space', in 'Interview', in Peter Buchanan, *Renzo Piano Building Workshop. Complete Works, II*, Phaidon, London 1995, pp. 64, 66. Richard Rogers played an important part in this development during the Beaubourg years: 'Then I was just an artisan, but with Richard I became an architect', in Renzo Piano, *La responsabilità dell'architetto*, Passigli, Florence 2004, p. 11. See also Thierry Paquot, 'Leçons d'urbanité', in *Renzo Piano, un regard construit*, Éditions du Centre Pompidou, Paris 2000, pp. 25–31.

[2] 'For someone like me, it's impossible to make a book of architecture. Also, I believe that an architect should say what he has to say through construction, not by making books', in *Renzo Piano, The Poetics of Construction*, School of Architecture and Planning, Massachusetts Institute of Technology, Cambridge (MA) 2002, p. 10.

[3] Renzo Piano, *Giornale di bordo*, Piano, Florence 2017, pp. 13–14.

[4] Renzo Piano, 'Il mestiere più antico del mondo', in *Micromega*, 2, 1996, p. 109. See also Renzo Piano, 'La mia piazza', in *Abitare le città. Genova 1492-1992*, monograph edition of *Abitare*, 311, 1991, p. 18

[5] In sequence: the District Laboratory on the Mole (1981), the metro station (1983–2003), the restoration of the Porto Antico (1985–2001), the masterplan for the Waterfront (2004), the Cetaceans Pavilion for the Aquarium (2007–2013), the pilots' tower (2014 and ongoing) and finally the masterplan for the eastern Waterfront (2020 and ongoing). See Andrea Plebe, 'Genova. Il futuro ha un cuore antico', in Fulvio Irace (ed.), *Renzo Piano Building Workshop. Le città visibili*, Triennale Electa, Milan 2007, pp. 45–51.

[6] See *Abitare le città*, op. cit, 1991; Peter Buchanan, *Renzo Piano Building Workshop. Complete Works, II*, Phaidon, London 1995, pp. 94–128; Lorenzo Ciccarelli, 'Mare e vento: Renzo Piano e Genova', in *Renzo Piano Building Workshop. Progetti d'acqua*, Renzo Piano Foundation, Genoa 2015, pp. 14–16.

[7] Biographical accounts of these young architects' careers with the Building Workshop are collected in the monographic 'Being Renzo Piano' edition of *Abitare*, 497, 2009. See also the author's conversation with Giorgio Grandi, Genoa, 29 July 2020. This participatory and collective dimension of the project emerges from an analysis of the plans and drawings kept at the Renzo Piano Foundation, Projects Archive, RPBW Collection, Redevelopment of the Porto Antico in Genoa 1985-2001.

[8] See Ennio Poleggi, 'La città e il mare', in *Abitare le città*, op. cit., pp. 50–54; Ennio Poleggi, Paolo Cevini, *Genova*, Laterza, Rome-Bari 2003.

[9] 'Genoa has had a deep impact on me. The port of Genoa, a place of balance and balancing acts, has taught me a lot', in *Renzo Piano 2002*, op. cit., p. 84.

[10] Uliano Lucas, *Vivere a Ponente*, Vangelista, Milan 1989; Antonio Gibelli, Paride Rugafiori (eds.), *La Liguria*, Einaudi, Turin 1994, pp. 257–290.

[11] Fabrizio De Miranda, 'Strada sopraelevata a Genova', in *Casabella*, 308, 1966, pp. 52–61.

[12] Renzo Piano, *Dialoghi di cantiere*, Laterza, Rome-Bari 1986, pp. 216–222.

[13] The RPBW began making studies of the Porto Antico area in 1984, the municipal authority formally commissioned the Building Workshop in the spring of 1985, and the plan was finalized by the Bureau International des Expositions in the following year. See Renzo Piano, 'Il progetto per l'Esposizione Colombiana del 1992 nel porto antico', in Paola Sirolli, Giovanni Battista Poggi, *Genova verso il 1992*, Municipality of Genoa, Genoa 1992, pp. 161–178.

[14] For a more general discussion of RPBW interventions on existing buildings, see Lorenzo Ciccarelli, 'Renzo Piano: Come conservare la memoria dei luoghi che cambiano?', in *Rassegna di Architettura e Urbanistica*, 145, 2015, pp. 59–64.

[15] The same observation would apply to the RPBW interventions in the Schlumberger workshops in Paris (1981–1984), the Lingotto building in Turin (1987–2002) or the transformation of the former Eridania sugar factory in Parma into the Paganini Auditorium (1997–2001).

16 The technical and curatorial planning of the Aquarium was entrusted to the American Cambridge Seven Associates practice, while Mark Carroll of the RPBW was responsible for the work on the building.

17 Renzo Piano, 'Il progetto per l'Esposizione Colombiana del 1992 nel porto antico', op. cit., pp. 168–169.

18 Regarding the long friendship and professional cooperation between Renzo Piano, Shunji Ishida and Sumusu Shingu, see Renzo Piano, 'Working With Shingu', in *Shingu. Message from Nature*, Abbeville, New York 1997, p. 17; Sumusu Shingu, 'Floating Architecture', in *Renzo Piano. The Art of Making Buildings*, Royal Academy of Arts, London 2018, pp. 117–120.

19 Federico Bucci, 'In the Age of Piano', in *Casabella*, 797, 2011, pp. 69–71.

20 See *Renzo Piano's Village for the Arts. Expansion of the High Museum of Art and Woodruff Arts Center*, High Museum of Art, Atlanta 2005; Peter Buchanan, *Renzo Piano Building Workshop. Complete Works, V*, Phaidon, London 2008, pp. 162–191.

21 Conversation between the author and Elisabetta Trezzani, Genoa, 25 May 2021. Overseeing the High Museum of Atlanta project was the first important task that Elisabetta Trezzani, now a Partner at the RPBW, took on when she joined the practice in the late 1990s.

22 Claudia Conforti, 'Auditorium di Renzo Piano a Roma', in Fulvio Irace (ed.) 2007, op. cit., pp. 99–105. See also Peter Buchanan 2008, op. cit., p. 12.

23 A dialogue between Meier and Piano concerning the enlargement of the High Museum was published as 'Atlanta: Renzo Piano dopo Richard Meier', in *Abitare*, 458, 2006, pp. 112–113.

24 Peter Buchanan 2008, op. cit., pp. 172–178. See also Edgar Stach, *Renzo Piano Building Workshop. Space-Detail-Light*, Birkhäuser, Basel 2021, pp. 74–81.

25 Kenneth Frampton, 'Renzo Piano e la Res Publica: Manhattan 2000–2008', in Fulvio Irace (ed.) 2007, op. cit., p. 27.

26 This quality was previously highlighted, in the late 1980s, by Reyner Banham, 'Making Architecture: The High Craft of Renzo Piano', in 'Renzo Piano Building Workshop: 1964–1988', in a+u, 3, 1989, p. 155.

27 Francesco Dal Co, *Renzo Piano*, Electa 2014, pp. 269–273.

28 Victoria Newhouse, 'Renzo Piano Alters the Character of New York's Morgan Library and Museum with a New Entrance and Skylit Court', in *The Architectural Record*, 10, 2006, p. 97.

29 Susanne Bauer, 'The Morgan Library and Museum, New York', in *Glas*, 1, 2007, pp. 22–23.

30 See Edgar Stach 2021, op. cit., pp. 90–101.

31 See Francesco Dal Co, 'Renzo Piano o dell'intelligenza efficace', in *Casabella*, 749, 2006, pp. 10–11.

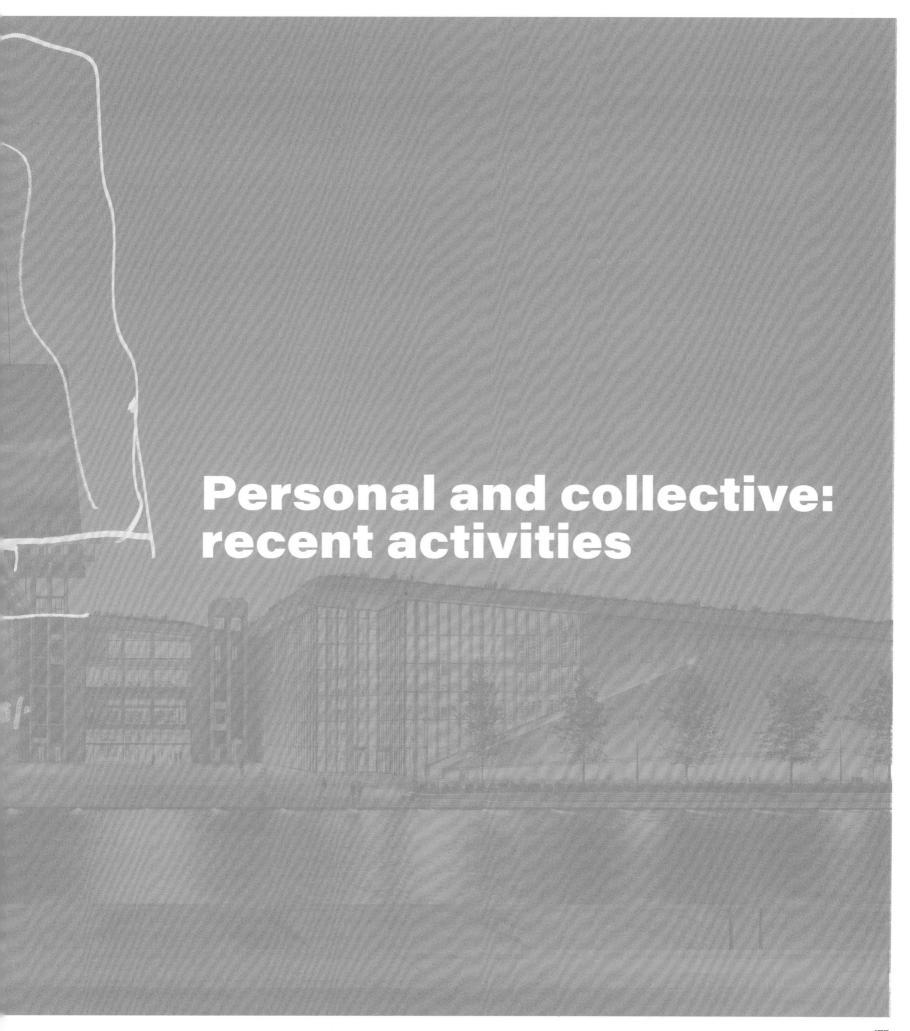

Personal and collective: recent activities

In the late 1980s, globalization and the whirlwind acceleration of production and communication systems brought about by CAD software and the internet substantially changed the character of architectural practices. These developments led to the emergence of companies operating on a global scale with offices on different continents and to new relationships between client, project and worksite.[1] These large practices adopted an industrial approach to their work, if only to maintain their economic and financial stability, impelled to conquer new markets by opening offices in the Gulf States and South-East Asia and to take on commissions likely to generate huge earnings, in particular large-scale infrastructure and residential and commercial development projects.[2] Having to organize the simultaneous inputs of several hundred (if not several thousand) staff members, while excessively enlarging the geographical scope of their interventions, giant enterprises of this kind have gradually abandoned both the time-honoured architect's office model and the Taylorist organization of work in which a few key figures with creative and decision-making powers were supported by a host of designer lackeys.[3]

In taking its place in the contemporary professional landscape, the Renzo Piano Building Workshop has only partially adopted these practices, having chosen a particularly interesting form of organization and project methodology.[4]

From the outset, Piano has created and carefully cultivated an international dimension, attested by his winning the commission for the Pompidou Centre and gradually extending this in the following decades to the United States, Japan and the southern hemisphere. His penchant for technical and constructional experimentation has enabled him to rapidly integrate innovations in IT and CAD/CAM into the planning methodology of his practice; this is a vital precondition for winning contracts to design infrastructure projects or large residential or office complexes.

The creations of the Building Workshop do not exhibit a single style that can be understood as a recurrent and recognizable architectural language. It is difficult to detect a stylistic relationship between, for example, the crystalline volumes of the Whitney Museum of American Art and the pierced-stone facades of the Maltese Parliament building, two of the most significant projects of the last decade. However, the two buildings are alike in sharing a profound concept, a rigour and a standard deriving from the tenacious application of a working method and a form of professional organization that have determined the secret of Piano's success over so many years.[5]

The Renzo Piano Building Workshop accepts no more than ten or twelve commissions at any one time. These are shared out among the Partners, who then form a project group consisting of a couple of associates and a similar number of architects.[6] This team will grow or decrease at different stages of the project and when building work actually starts. Teams do not work in isolation but rather under a system of communicating vessels: the Partners or associates working on one project may at the same time monitor a second and contribute by inputting their own ideas.[7]

Renzo Piano, meanwhile, is the orchestral conductor: the only person in the Building Workshop who supervises and contributes to all the current projects. Until the advent of the pandemic his monthly diary was organized as follows: one week in the Genoa studio, two weeks in Paris and the rest of the time out on site inspections.

This overall coordinating role is reflected in the careful 'planning' of his work station.[8] In particular in the Punta Nave studio, built on steep terracing overlooking the sea far below, Piano's huge work table occupies a strategic position, visible from all points.[9] On the adjacent wall, bundles of sketches drawn in green felt-tip – one for each current project – are held by a neat series of bulldog clips: Piano's notes and insights as each project develops. A similar wall of sketchpads watches over Piano's desk in the Paris studio. These collections of drawings are available to all the architects working in the office, enabling them to check the progress of each project.[10]

While sketches are a project's detailed background material, they are complemented by so-called 'reference images': the visuals around which the first raw ideas for a project accumulate. These are the photographs, reproductions, engravings, newspaper clippings and so on that become intuitively associated with a given project, for which they serve as constant points of reference. The reference images express the key idea, the concept, that inspires the project, ensuring that the architects never lose sight of it.[11]

Reference images might be, for example, Max Berg's Jahrhunderthalle/Centennial Hall in Wrocław for the Padre Pio Church at San Giovanni Rotondo, on account of its complex structure of flying buttresses; Georges Seurat's painting of the Grande Jatte for the Art Institute of Chicago, on account of the rarefied light required in the exhibition galleries; the front doors and colourful signs of London pubs and dwellings for the Central St Giles Court in London, on account of the vivid colours of the building's facade; or the 1616 engraving by Claes Jansz Visscher of the spires of London seen from Southwark for The Shard, on account of the sharp, pointed profile of the skyscraper.[12]

These sketches and reference images are the wellsprings of Piano's work, triggered by visits to project locations – the first and inescapable step for every commission.

The continuous interaction between Piano and 'his' architects is reflected in a particular type of sketch in which Piano asks questions and seeks confirmation or critical comment on the quality of

THE SHARD, PLAN OF THE NINTH FLOOR, HOUSING OFFICES.

his intuitions. The rigorous practice of 'listening to the location' and the uninterrupted dialogue between Piano and the Partners – which covers the whole project management process and continues on the worksite – are the two modes of operation that prevent the Building Workshop from tritely repeating a particular formula. This is evident from an examination of some of the dozens of projects completed in the last twenty years: from major projects such as the London Shard (2000–2012), the Stavros Niarchos Cultural Foundation in Athens (2008–2016) and the design of the City Gate and new Parliament Building in Valletta (2009–2015), to smaller projects occasioned by circumstances of acute need, such as the Auditorium del Parco in L'Aquila (2010–2012) and EMERGENCY's Children's Surgical Hospital in Entebbe, Uganda (2013–2020).

0 2 4   10 m
  1   3   5

► In 1998 Renzo Piano was awarded the Pritzker Architecture Prize, a distinction that amplified his reputation and prestige, especially in the English-speaking world, where in the following decade he was given opportunities to plan and construct many public and private buildings. It was no coincidence that in 2000 the Renzo Piano Building Workshop was entrusted with commissions to design two skyscrapers, a type of building that had hitherto remained marginal to the work of his practice: the New York Times headquarters (2000–2007) and The Shard in London. These two landmark projects boosted the RPBW's credit with the major American and British institutions and developers, which have ever since made almost a habit of turning to the Genoa/Paris-based practice.[13]

Irvine Sellar asked Renzo Piano to design a new tower to be built in London, in an area charged with historic memories – as well as planning and infrastructural complexities. The irregular site, devastated by German bombing during World War II, was in the Borough of Southwark, between London Bridge Station and St Thomas Street, one of the city's most ancient streets and the traditional access to London Bridge.

For the London skyscraper, as with the New York Times project, Piano, RPBW Partner Joost Moolhuijzen and his co-workers paid special attention to the way such an imposing building would fit into the cityscape, focusing on two key aspects: its anchorage at ground level, and how to fragment, break up and lighten the volume of the tower itself.

At street level the architects agreed with the client to subtract as much private space as possible from the tower and devote it to public functions, while the lower levels of The Shard are raised off the ground and sheltered by a series of glass canopies, arranged horizontally at different heights, so as to preserve the human scale of St Thomas Street and the district generally.[14] The RPBW project also extended to the new entrance to London Bridge Station and, in more recent years, to the design and execution of two other – smaller – buildings

THE RAILWAY LINES SNAKING OUT FROM LONDON BRIDGE STATION AND, TO THE LEFT, THE RIVER THAMES.

that stand alongside The Shard: The News Building (2004–2013) and Shard Place (2013–2023), thus giving architectural and urban consistency to this part of the city.

As with the New York skyscraper, the corners of The Shard are 'desegregated': rather than being clearly defined, they are designed to resemble an irregular hexagonal plant that narrows as it reaches for the sky.[15] The name 'Shard' emerged from Piano's very first sketches; he imagined the tower as a slender, sharp, serrated structure: a crystal dissolving into the London sky. Three hundred and ten metres in height, The Shard covers a ground area of 4,000 metres square, while at its summit the viewing platform is only 350 metres square. Seen from street level or from the Thames, the tower appears to be enclosed in a series of non-contiguous glass slivers, open at the summit as if to scratch the clouds with their sharp outlines.

The decision in favour of entirely glazed elevations, and the many experiments to enhance the quality and finish of the glass, were a consequence of the intention to dematerialize the imposing mass of the skyscraper against the changing London sky, to reflect the nuanced changes of the light at different times of day and seasons of the year.

TOP: THE CANOPIES CONNECTING THE MONUMENTAL STAIRWAY OF THE SHARD TO THOSE LEADING TO THE STREET AND THE SURROUNDING BUILDINGS.
ABOVE: GROUND PLAN OF THE SHARD ALONGSIDE THE RAILWAY LINES OF LONDON BRIDGE STATION.
OPPOSITE: ONE OF THE DISJOINED GLASS SPIKES OF THE SKYSCRAPER.

The Shard has a double facade, or double skin, with two screens of glass sandwiching a 20-centimetre cavity housing roll-down blinds.[16] This double facade greatly improves the energy performance of the building and has made it possible to use 'extra-white' glass for the outer skin, the reduced ferrous-oxide content of this raw material giving the building its crystalline appearance.[17] The external panels are made using a 'float-glass' technique, producing an extremely flat effect compared to the conventional tempered processing method, which gives the glass a ripple effect. As is often the case with Piano's projects, technological research and experimentation with materials tend to ensure not only durability and efficient performance but, above all, the realization of the ideas provisionally highlighted in the initial sketches. Painstaking attention to detail and the desire to match a building modestly with its urban setting complement and support each other throughout the design and construction process.

RIGHT: THE SHARD'S
ENTRANCE LOBBY.
OPPOSITE PAGE: THE SHARP,
CRYSTALLINE PROFILE OF THE
SKYSCRAPER SET AGAINST
THE THAMES.

► Commissioned directly by Andreas Dracopoulos, nephew of the wealthy Greek shipowner Stavros Niarchos, the new headquarters for the foundation dedicated to his uncle was intended as an expression of love for Athens and Greece, at a time when the country was suffering a serious economic crisis. The building provided the city with a new theatre and with more capacious and technological premises for the national library, at the same time recovering an area in the vicinity of the Phaleron, site of Athens' original harbour, which had been neglected since the 2004 Olympic Games[18].

The interest of the project lies not so much in the precise and convincing planning of the theatre, the concert halls, the library with its teaching workshops and the myriad other areas making up the complex – one would expect no less from a practice as experienced as the Building Workshop and its tried-and-tested consultants and employees – but rather in the fact that, once again, the request for a project of this kind was interpreted as an opportunity for shaping a new public space, not necessarily requested by the client, and as serving to reconnect the area, materially and in people's perceptions, with the sea and the rest of the city.

RENZO PIANO'S SKETCHES IMMEDIATELY
GIVE BODILY FORM TO THE IDEAS THAT
WILL UNDERPIN A PROJECT. THOSE
BEHIND THE NEW BUILDING FOR THE
STAVROS NIARCHOS FOUNDATION IN
ATHENS WERE: RECONNECTING WITH THE
SEA; THE LARGE, OPEN NEIGHBOURHOOD
PARK; AND THE NEW SQUARE AT THE
HEART OF THE PROJECT.

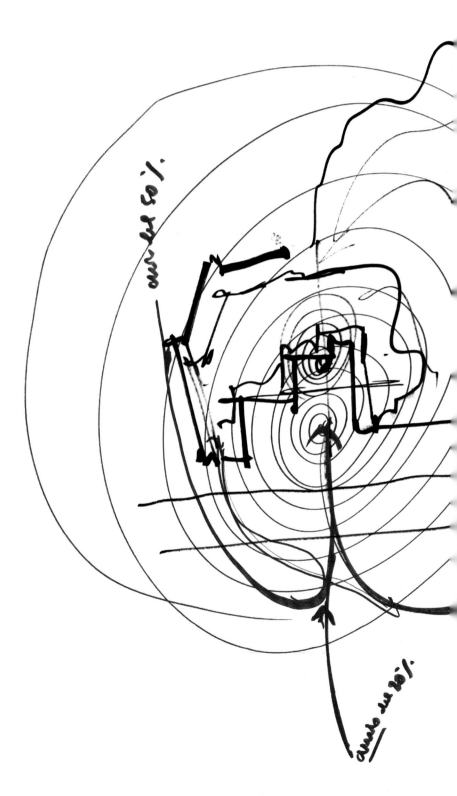

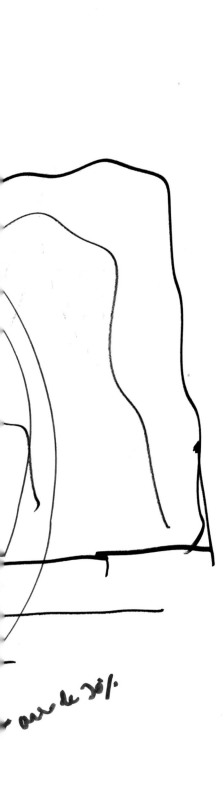

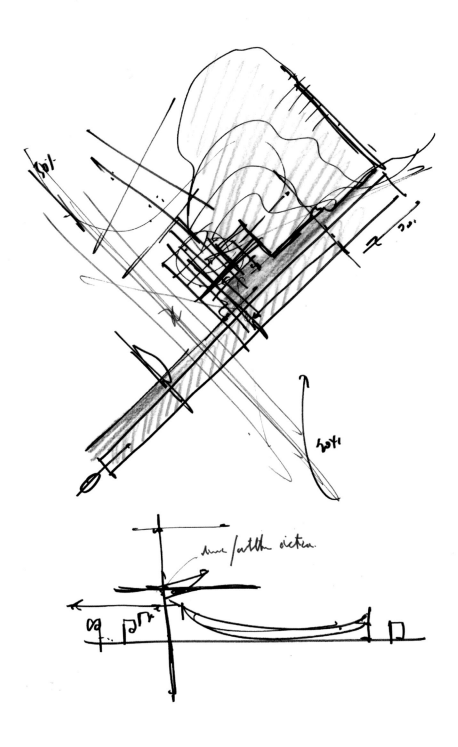

THE PLAN SHOWS THE LARGE
SCALE OF THE NEW PARK SERVING
THIS PERIPHERAL AREA OF ATHENS,
WITH THE MAGNIFICENT VIEW
OF PHALERON HARBOUR WHICH
CAN BE ENJOYED FROM ITS
HIGHEST POINT.

192

The crucial moment during the first site inspection was when Renzo Piano and Giorgio Bianchi – the Partner in charge – climbed to the top floor of a residential building on the edge of the area, from which there was a magnificent view of the sweep of the harbour and, at their backs, the Acropolis.[19] The cultural centre was therefore planned with a topographical intervention in mind: the creation of an artificial hill (using spoil from motorway and underground tunnels) so that visitors, having climbed to the top, could enjoy the same view and be less aware of the peripheral nature of the site. The re-creation of a close relationship with the sea was the inspiration for a second topological intervention: the cutting of a canal – 400 metres in length and 30 metres wide – to bring seawater right into the heart of the project. Finally, squeezed between the canal and the hill, Piano decided

to include an 'agora', a new open space 40 metres square giving access to the different parts of the cultural centre.

The opera house and the national library, for which the project was originally conceived, are out of sight, hidden beneath the artificial hill.[20] Instead, Piano's emphasis was on the public spaces: the park, the navigable canal, the walkway and the square that adjoin the centre. On the summit of the hill, towards the bay, floats a huge 100-metre-square roof structure: the so-called 'solar canopy', supported on slender 17-metre-high steel columns. This is a hollow structure constructed of two thin

shells of ferrocement: the upper shell supports one hectare of solar panels producing roughly 2.5 megawatt hours of electricity, sufficient for the basic needs of the building, while the lower shell shelters a large panoramic terrace, which also accommodates a reading room.

Access is via the park, which is 170,000 metres square in area and planted with some 1,500 trees and 200,000 bushes native to the Mediterranean: Maremma pines, Greek olives, shrubs from Puglia, forming the strategic hub of the whole intervention. Walking slowly up the 500-metre approach, visitors reach a height of 32 metres and, suspended

THE ROOF OF THE CULTURAL
CENTRE FLOATS ON SLENDER
STEEL COLUMNS AT THE HIGH
END OF THE PARK, LIKE A GLIDER
ABOUT TO TAKE OFF.

ACCESS TO THE VARIOUS AREAS OF
THE CULTURAL CENTRE IS VIA THE
'AGORA', THE NEW OPEN SPACE
SQUEEZED BETWEEN THE CANAL
AND THE GLAZED FACADES OF
THE BUILDING.

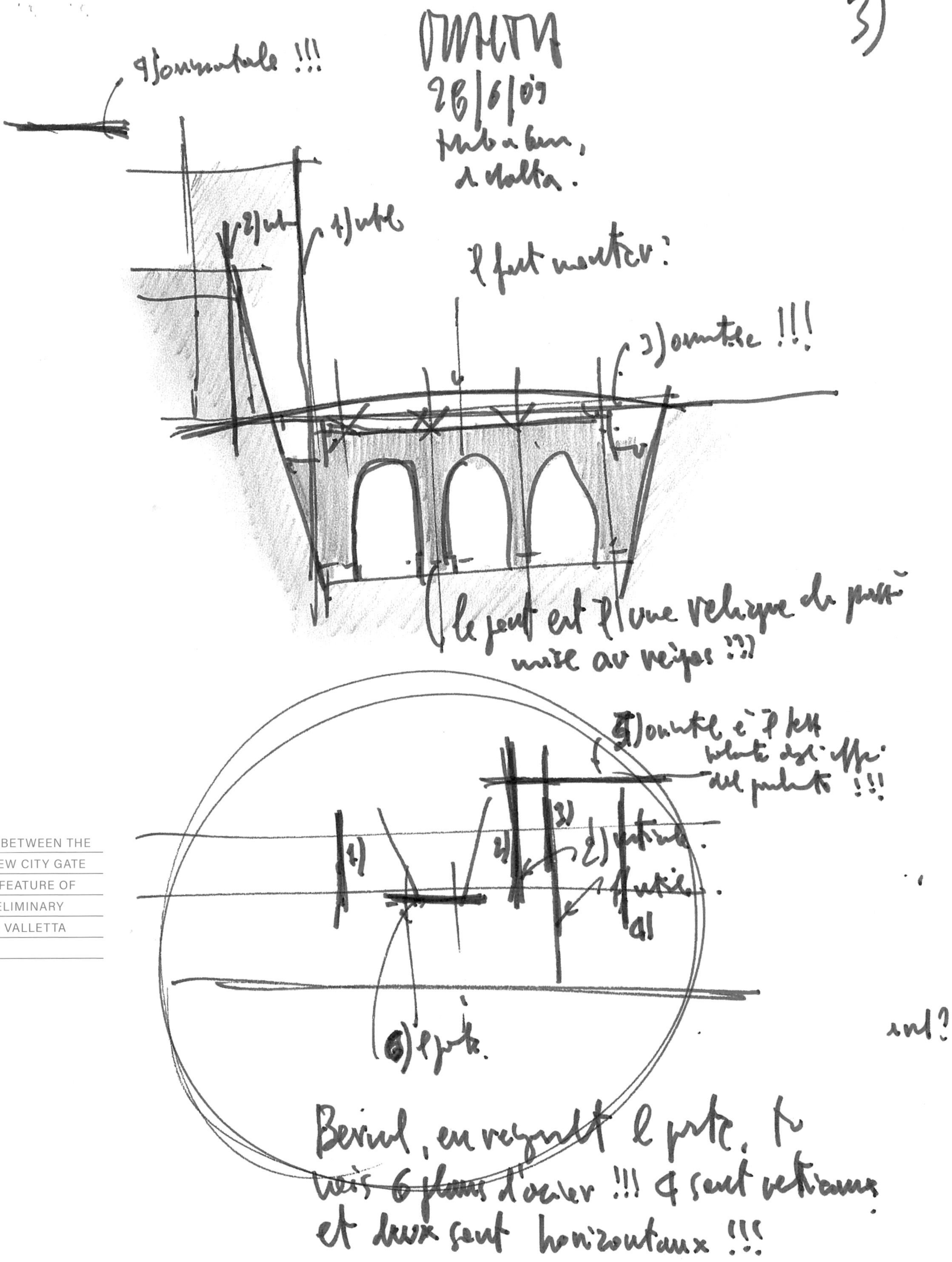

THE RELATIONSHIP BETWEEN THE
BRIDGE AND THE NEW CITY GATE
WAS THE CENTRAL FEATURE OF
RENZO PIANO'S PRELIMINARY
SKETCHES FOR THE VALLETTA
PROJECT, 2009.

RIGHT: THIS SKETCH EXPLORES
THE SENSATIONS OF COMPRESSION
AND DECOMPRESSION THAT
THE VISITOR EXPERIENCES
WHILE PASSING THROUGH
THE DIFFERENT PARTS OF THE
VALLETTA DEVELOPMENT: FROM
THE BRIDGE TO THE CITY GATE,
FROM PARLIAMENT SQUARE TO THE
INTERIOR OF THE OPERA HOUSE.

between sea and sky, are immersed in the fragrance of sage, bay laurel, almond, pomegranate and rosemary, while shaded by olives and cypresses.[21]

▶ The same idea of an architectural project as a way of conducting extensive planning operations to reconstitute and reconnect down-at-heel city areas was behind the commission entrusted to the Renzo Piano Building Workshop to restore the City Gate area of Valletta, as well as to design a new Parliament building.[22]

Piano had already studied the area in 1986, when UNESCO asked him to restore this entry point to the old city, which had been subject to many overlapping interventions over the centuries. Here there is a bridge that was carrying traffic across a moat, thus linking the spacious *piazzale* that also served as the bus station with the ancient city walls and old town. When in 2008 the Great Harbour Regeneration Corporation again invited Piano to Malta, his earlier studies provided the basis for the new project, carried out in conjunction with Partners Bernard Plattner and Antonio Belvedere.

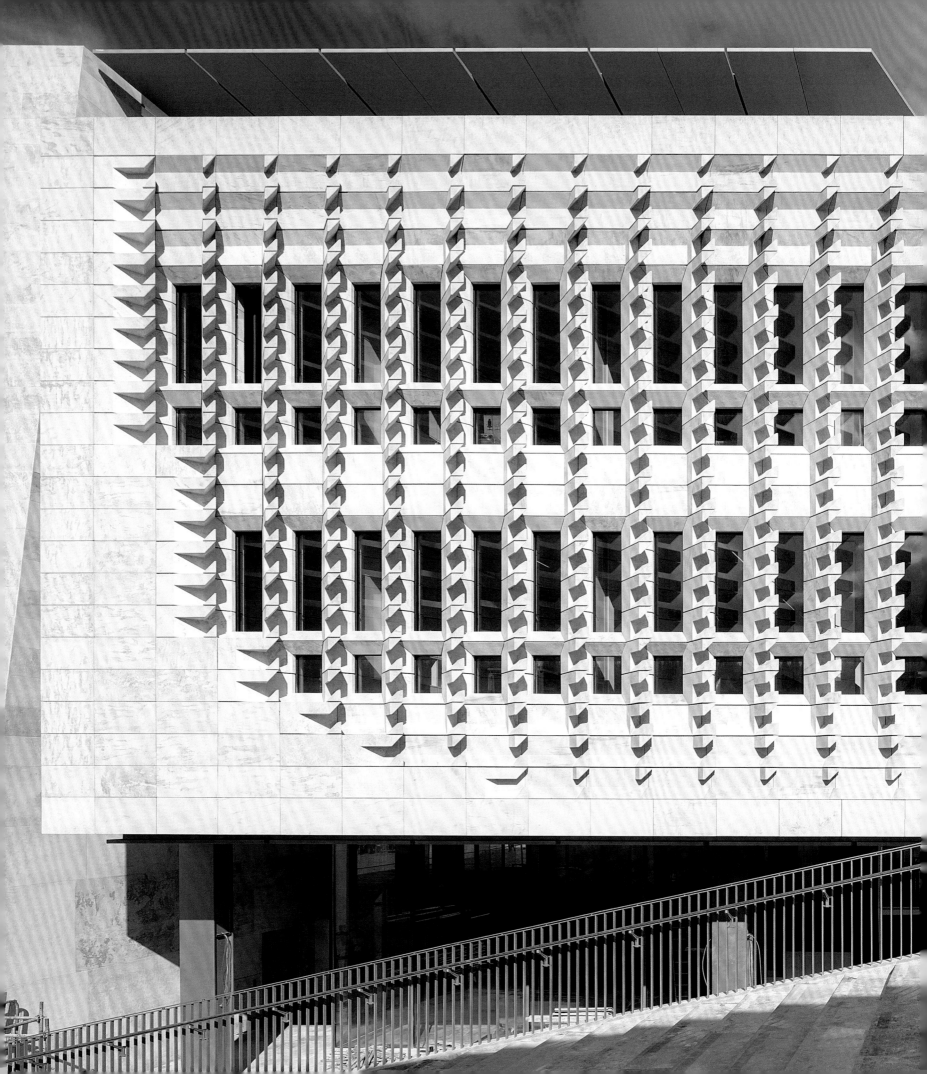

Experimentation with materials as the generative element of his work has always been a typical aspect of Renzo Piano's career, from the first lightweight structures he designed in the 1960s to his most recent town planning projects.

It was first decided to return the bridge to its original dimensions, as designed by Dingli in 1633, get rid of the traffic and pedestrianize it. Conjoined to the bridge is a new gate, open to the sky and with massive blocks of stone on either side, and upright steel spears positioned to clearly define the border line between the old and the new. It was decided to interrupt the stretch of road that ran above the City Gate and create two monumental stairways backing onto it, thus opening up a new pedestrian route connecting the two monumental bastions, which were then converted into exhibition venues.

The local stone – an unusual material of which Piano had little experience – is the real star of the entire project, giving unity to its different components. After some thorough research by the Building Workshop architects, a new quarry was opened on the neighbouring island of Gozo to supply stone of the yellowish hue typical of Malta's historic buildings. While the City Gate required the use of this stone on a massive scale, the new Parliament building provides a vibrant technological interpretation of it.

The client wished to site the new Parliament building over the ruins of the Opera House, which had been destroyed by the saturation bombing inflicted on the island during World War II. Piano, Bernard Plattner and Antonio Belvedere quickly realized that this solution would deprive the Maltese of the memory of a

building with which an important part of the modern history of the city was associated.[23]

Having convinced the client of the virtue of a different solution for the area, the architects decided to reinstate the Opera House, the ruins of which have been preserved, and use them as foundation for a new theatrical complex designed in conjunction with Daniele Abbado. It consists of two banks of wooden seating and a lightweight steel structure equipped with lighting and sound systems to create an open-air theatre capable of holding an audience of one thousand.[24]

The Parliament building was instead located on a plot between the City Gate and the Opera House, facing onto a new public square, 60 x 25 metres, opened up by transforming Freedom Street, previously used as a car park, and demolishing two buildings abutting the

Auberge d'Italie and the Church of Santa Caterina. The result was a coherent sequence of architectural phenomena – the bridge, the gate, the Parliament building with its adjoining square and the Opera House – ushering the visitor into the historic heart of Valletta.

The Parliament building consists of two apparently sun-baked stone-clad blocks supported on steel columns set back 11 metres from their facades, creating a sense of lightness as if they were hanging in the air.

Sections of these stone blocks were pierced and shaped by digitally controlled machinery so

as to filter the solar radiation and provide natural lighting for the rooms within. The elevations of the building match the Baroque character of many of Valletta's historic buildings in a contemporary key. As is often the case with Piano's creations, the built mass has been broken down into several components, separate but adjacent, so that the public space of the square penetrates the ground floor areas, passes through the building and gives unity to the new square, the building itself and the surrounding streets.

THE LOCATION OF THE AUDITORIUM
DEL PARCO, IN THE HEART OF THE
CITY OF L'AQUILA, BATTERED BY THE
EARTHQUAKE, WAS A DETERMINING
FACTOR OF THE PROJECT, LONG
STUDIED BY PIANO.

► While the vast scenic undertakings of Athens and Valletta are testimony to the well-established capacity of the Renzo Piano Building Workshop to tackle cultural and political projects, acting in the wider context of sensitive urban and suburban contexts, in recent years Renzo Piano has also set aside time to work on small-scale projects. These are often the outcome of personal friendships, as for example with Claudio Abbado (1933–2014) and Gino Strada (1948–2021). Projects of this kind do not fill the coffers of the Building Workshop but are undertaken by Piano himself, sometimes with the help of former colleagues or architects not associated with the practice.

Quite apart from other damage, the ruinous earthquake of 6 April 2009 deprived the people of L'Aquila in central Italy of many of the music venues that had been such a feature of the old city.[25] Immediately after the disaster, Claudio Abbado – who had featured in and conducted concerts there as a young virtuoso and had always maintained feelings of gratitude and affection for the city – involved Piano in designing a new temporary auditorium. For many years L'Aquila had no music venue to call its own or public buildings generally, which were sorely lacking in the so-called 'new settlements'. Abbado wanted to heal this wound and Piano agreed to lend him a hand.[26]

An interest in music, friendships with composers, conductors and musicians, and the planning of music venues have been a constant thread running through Renzo Piano's life and career.

The construction of a new auditorium was made possible by generous funding from the Autonomous Province of Trento, which provided a large supply of valuable timber from the Val di Fiemme as well as covering the costs of the work. Contrary to usual Building Workshop practice, the project was drawn up by Renzo Piano personally, the only other input being from associate architect Paolo Colonna. He also looked for help to Alessandro Traldi, who had worked with him in Genoa in the 1980s.[27]

Piano, Colonna and Traldi took their time in choosing a location for the auditorium: unusually, the site had not been officially designated but was chosen by the architects, in consultation with the municipal authorities.[28]

A simpler solution, and one which might have ensured immediate results, would have been to choose a site on the city outskirts, maybe close to the residential settlements built for those who had lost their homes. However, Abbado and Piano's objective was not to get things up and running immediately but rather to encourage the resettlement of the old town, not to abandon the neighbourhoods devastated by the earthquake but to facilitate their gradual reappropriation by local people. Given that the whole city centre had been declared a red zone – and remained so for almost ten years, the architects chose a site on the slopes of the Forte Spagnolo, near the Piazza della Fontana Luminosa, which in the first months after the earthquake was one of the city's few partially active areas, enlivened by one of the Civil Defence centres and the only bar still open for business.[29]

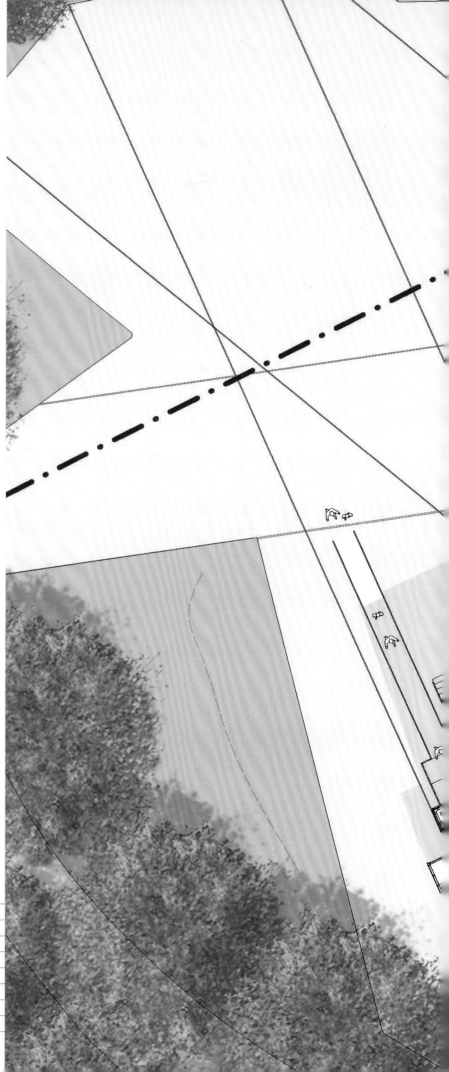

THE AUDITORIUM DEL PARCO
CONSISTS OF THREE SQUARE
BUILDINGS CLAD WITH STRIPS OF
WOOD. THE AUDITORIUM ITSELF
OCCUPIES THE MIDDLE BLOCK,
WHILE THE TWO LATERAL BUILDINGS
HOUSE THE ENTRANCE AND
FOYER, THE DRESSING ROOMS
AND BACKSTAGE AREAS.

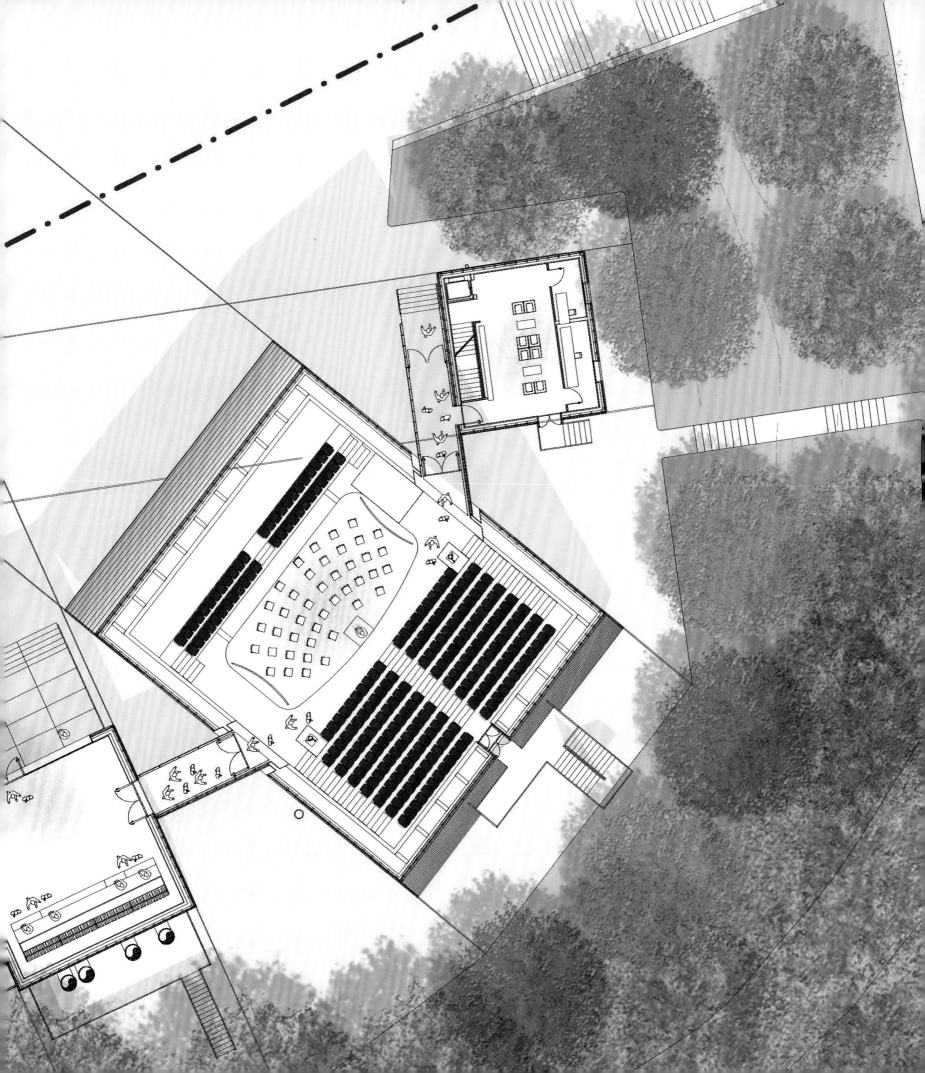

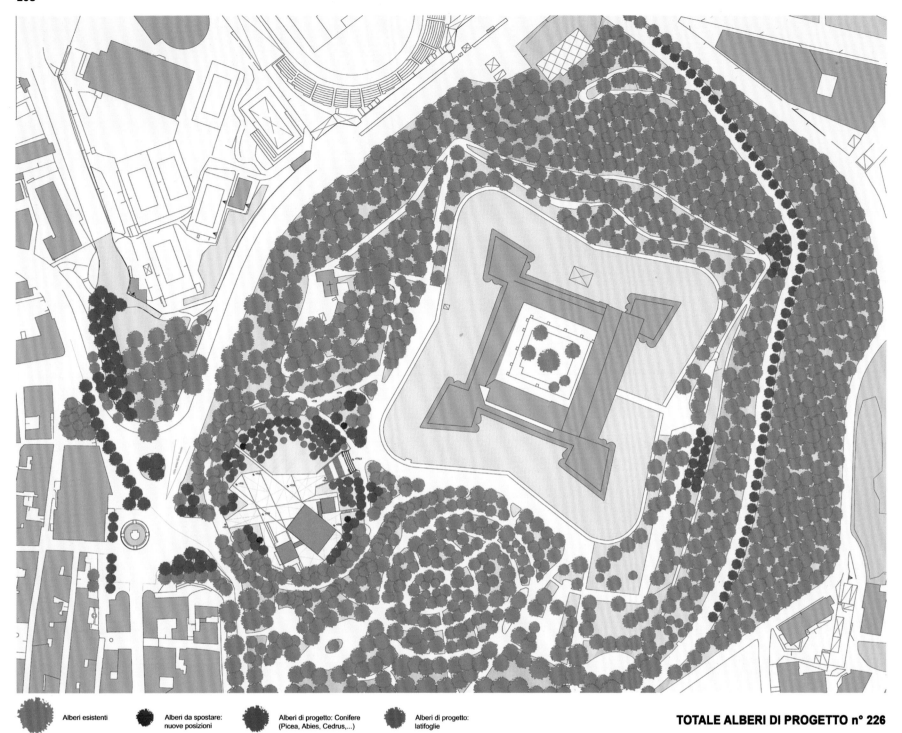

Alberi esistenti

Alberi da spostare: nuove posizioni

Alberi di progetto: Conifere (Picea, Abies, Cedrus,...)

Alberi di progetto: latifoglie

TOTALE ALBERI DI PROGETTO n° 226

The Auditorium del Parco – as it soon came to be known – consists of three cube-like buildings connected by narrow walkways made of iron, glass and wood. The largest building, 19 metres square, seemingly dug into the ground at an angle of 30 degrees, houses a concert hall holding 40 musicians and 238 spectators. The seating inside the building backs onto the sloping walls to ensure an optimal view of the stage. The two smaller cubes, to the left and right of the main building, house the services, the technical installations and the artists' dressing rooms. The auditorium is entered from the two smaller buildings via the walkways.

ABOVE: STRATEGICALLY POSITIONED BETWEEN THE FORTE SPAGNOLO AND THE PIAZZA DELLA FONTANA LUMINOSA, THE AUDITORIUM DEL PARCO MARKS ONE OF THE MAIN ENTRANCES TO THE OLD CITY CENTRE OF L'AQUILA.

RIGHT: THE COLOURFUL NARROW WOODEN BOARDS THAT CLAD THE ENTIRETY OF THE AUDITORIUM BUILDINGS STAND OUT AMONG THE TREES OF THE PARK, IN THIS CASE IN THE SNOW THAT OFTEN CARPETS THE CITY IN WINTER.

THE STRATEGY OF
'DISCONNECTION', OR DIVIDING
A COMPLEX INTO SEVERAL
SEPARATE COMPONENTS, ALSO
CHARACTERIZES RENZO PIANO'S
L'AQUILA PROJECT.

With the sole exception of the reinforced-concrete base of the concert hall, which is supported on sixteen concrete pillars with elastomeric insulators, the structure of the building is entirely of timber donated by the Province of Trento.[30] Timber complies with the strictest anti-seismic standards and also makes it possible to dismantle the three cubes if ever the Auditorium del Parco were to be moved to another location once the concert hall in the Forte Spagnola is fully restored.

The wooden boards are distinguished by a particular colour, less saturated in the middle sections of each elevation, more vivid towards the corners. Different shades of red, orange, green, purple, pink and light-blue rise one upon another, blurring the outlines of the buildings and causing them to blend in with the greens, yellows and reds of the surrounding vegetation.[31]

Inaugurated on 7 October 2012 with a concert by the Mozart Orchestra under the baton of Claudio Abbado, over the years the small building has exceeded its original function: for many years the only public venue in the historic centre of L'Aquila, it has been used for meetings, debates and even weddings, as well as for concerts and entertainments of various kinds.[32]

▶ The recently inaugurated Children's Surgical Hospital in Entebbe is also the fruit of a long-standing friendship.[33] In 2013 Gino Strada asked Renzo Piano if he would design a new paediatric

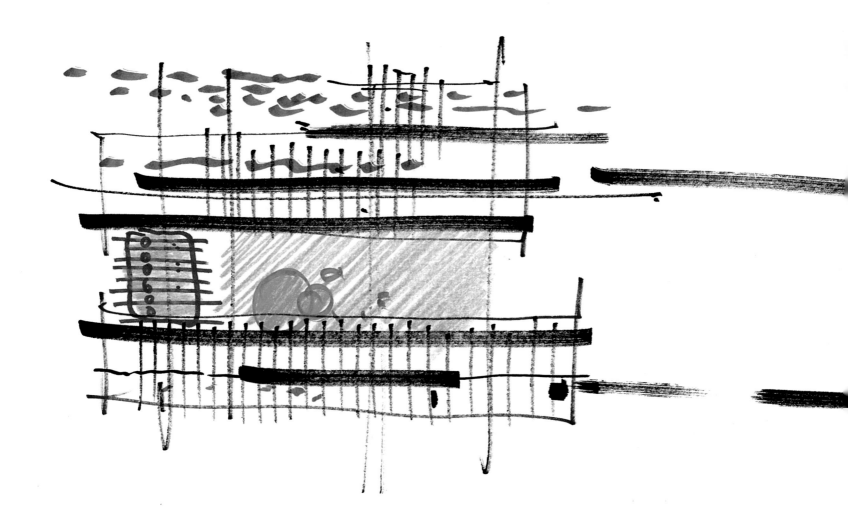

centre in Uganda. The site is strategically located on the northern shore of Lake Victoria thirty or so miles from the capital, Kampala, and easily reached from some of Africa's most notorious killing fields: the Congo, Rwanda and South Sudan, as well as from Tanzania and Kenya.

EMERGENCY, the NGO founded in 1994, has been outstanding over the years not only in its tireless commitment to bringing free and high-quality health care to some of the most violent areas of conflict, without discriminating on the grounds of nationality or political affiliation, but also for the strange 'beauty' of its hospitals – a further way of mitigating suffering. Most of these projects have been carried out by TAMassociati, a practice based in Venice.[34] So for Renzo Piano's Entebbe hospital project, in which he was assisted by Building Workshop Partner Giorgio Grandi, he also cooperated with TAMassociati architects.[35]

Hospitals tend to be buildings both complex and simple: their layout is almost entirely dictated by an enormous number of regulatory and safety-related stipulations, and by the high standards of performance they are expected to deliver.

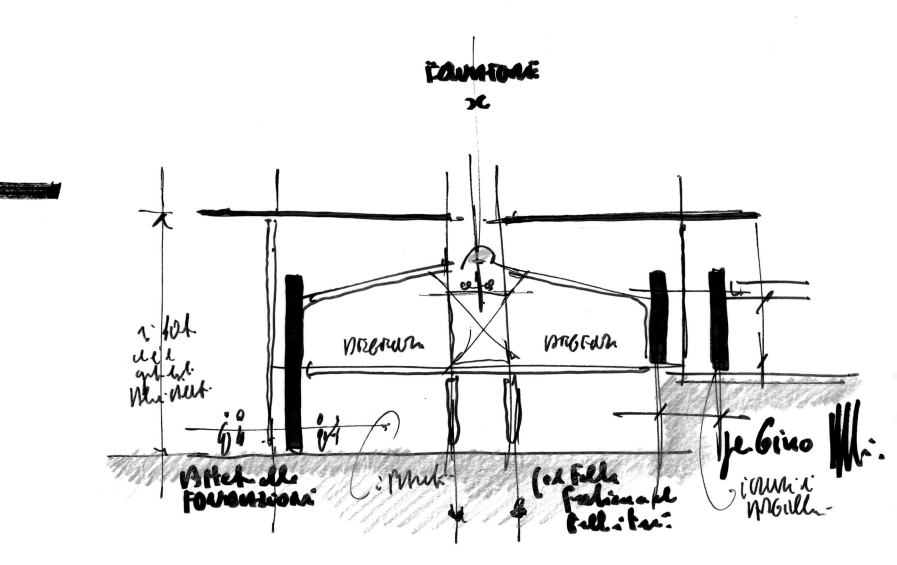

THE RATIONAL DESIGN OF
EMERGENCY'S CHILDREN'S
SURGICAL HOSPITAL IN ENTEBBE
REFLECTS THE BARE-ESSENTIALS
QUALITY OF LIFE IN UGANDA, AND
THE INEVITABLY LIMITED BUDGET,
IN AN ENTIRELY POSITIVE WAY.

1155.25

1157.50

58.00

58.50

115

1159

116

116

118

116

1152.50

163.50

1164.00

4.50

1165.00

1165.50

65.00

5.50
6.00

6.50

67

8.50

WARD DEPARTEMENT

I.C.U.

O.T. DEPARTEMENT

DIAGNOSTIC

ENTRANCE

N

The Uganda project therefore also began with a pains-taking study of the hospital's various functions, and the need for them to be carefully differentiated and immediately identifiable.

The layout towards which the architects naturally gravitated – simple, functional and flexible – features seven parallel walls, this layout having previously served as the backbone for a number of Renzo Piano's projects: the Nasher Sculpture Center in Dallas (1999–2003) and the Fondation Beyeler (1991–1997) in Basel, to cite just two examples.

Two wings – one housing the wards with 72 beds, the other the reception area, clinics and day services – are joined by a central block containing the three operating theatres. The two long wings, which at basement level accommodate storerooms and service areas, are joined at ground-floor level by a connecting walkway and a luxuriant garden that leads the eye away into the meadows and surrounding vegetation and on towards Lake Victoria in the distance.

The seven 60-centimetre-thick walls that define the architecture of the Children's Hospital are made of rammed earth, an unusual technique for the Building Workshop and never before used on this scale. The choice of material was dictated by various factors, above all the difficulty in finding more modern building materials locally and the skilled labour to work with them. Following EMERGENCY's established practice,

THE ENTRANCE AREA, WARDS
AND THEATRE BLOCK ARE
LOCATED IN DIFFERENT PARTS
OF THE BUILDING, BUT UNITED
BY A TRANSVERSE WALKWAY AND
LINKED TOGETHER BY THE GARDEN.

FOLLOWING DOUBLE PAGE: THE
CHILDREN'S HOSPITAL, WITH LAKE
VICTORIA IN THE BACKGROUND.

THE SOLID WEIGHT OF THE
RAMMED-EARTH WALLS IS
COUNTERBALANCED BY THE
LIGHTNESS OF THE METAL
COLUMNS AND THE ROOF.

the hospital worksite was intended to be a building school for local workers, teaching them techniques that they could redeploy at other times and in other places. The decision to use the quintessential local building material, clay, and adopt the most basic procedures was therefore an ethical decision, as well as a pragmatic one.[36]

The long walls of the hospital were made by mixing local clay with aggregates and reagents that would improve its mechanical strength and prevent it from being washed away, compacting layers of the compound one upon another within a metal framework.[37] This rammed earth, with its granular structure and streaks of colour ranging from brown to orange to red, is the defining feature of the hospital, and the two hundred people from the surrounding villages who took part in its construction were subsequently recruited for the hospital's cleaning and maintenance departments.

The walls are punctuated by a series of rectangular openings, while above them floats a roof of standard circular steel sections and thin metal sheets, which are like a butterfly's wings opening. Below this upper layer, which is fitted with some 2,500 photovoltaic panels, a more robust roof shelters the various areas of the hospital, while glazed screens close off the two wings of the building and the intermediate walkways. The colours and living tapestry of the trees, the forest, the meadows and the lake seem to penetrate the hospital, while the skylights in the two wings ensure that the interiors are naturally lit.

The decision to end this crossing of the *mare magnum* of Renzo Piano projects with two smaller-scale works dictated by emergency circumstances like the L'Aquila auditorium and the Entebbe children's hospital is no coincidence.

In the introduction to this book, I tried to plot an ideal course taken by the Genoese architect (and master navigator): setting sail with a love of technical experimentation and the skilful

FOLLOWING DOUBLE PAGE: LOCAL
CLAY MIXED WITH AGGREGATES
WAS USED TO FORM THE HOSPITAL'S
MASSIVE WALLS, WHICH ALSO
INSULATE THE WARDS AND CLINICS
AGAINST EXCESSIVE HEAT.

Large-scale urban interventions and smaller more jewel-like projects would seem to be the two poles of the RPBW's recent creativity.

assembly of materials and ending his voyage in a mature relationship with urban and natural settings dictated by a desire to reconnect the threads and create public space.

In the vast and multifaceted production of the Renzo Piano Building Workshop, which must necessarily accept and in some cases adapt to existing typological, spatial and constructional solutions, the Auditorium del Parco and the Children's Surgical Hospital bear witness to the fact that this voyage is ongoing, and that the best of the practice's production continues to spring from the meeting of the personal and collective dimensions of its work.

A WING OF THE HOSPITAL, SHOWING
THE METAL ROOF STRUCTURE.

GIORGIO GRANDI, GINO STRADA AND PAUL
PANTALAO OF TAMASSOCIATI, RENZO PIANO AND
SOME OF THE PEOPLE WORKING ON THE PROJECT
STAND IN FRONT OF A MOCK-UP OF ONE OF THE
WALLS OF THE NEW HOSPITAL.

1 See, for example, Phillip Bernstein, *Architecture Design Data. Practice Competency in the Era of Computation*, Birkhäuser, Basel 2018; Lorenzo Ciccarelli, Sara Lombardi, Lorenzo Mingardi (eds.), Largest Architectural Firms. Design Authorship and Organization Management, Edifir, Florence 2021.

2 Global Design. International Perspectives and Individual Concepts, Lars Müller, Basel 2010.

3 Peggy Deamer, Phillip Bernstein (eds.), *Building (in) the Future. Recasting Labor in Architecture*, Princeton Architectural Press, New York 2010.

4 See Lorenzo Ciccarelli, 'Un architetto e il suo studio: Renzo Piano (e) Building Workshop', in Sergio Russo Ermolli, Giuliano Galluccio, *Materia, Prodotto, Dato. Il valore dell'informazione nelle architetture del Renzo Piano Building Workshop*, Maggioli, Sant'Arcangelo di Romagna 2021, pp. 171–176.

5 The general indifference to Renzo Piano's style, rooted in a planning method both rigorous and open to contributions from Building Workshop members, has been highlighted by Kenneth Frampton in his Preface to *Renzo Piano, Giornale di bordo*, Passigli, Florence 1997, p. 7.

6 Conversation between the author and Philippe Goubet, Paris, 30 November 2018.

7 Conversation between the author and Elisabetta Trezzani, Genoa, 21 October 2021.

8 Claudia Conforti, 'Renzo Piano, un architecte à l'écoute de la ville', in *ArtItalies*, 21, 2015, pp. 145–151.

9 Claudia Conforti, 'La fiamma e il cristallo: due percorsi nell'architettura di Renzo Piano', in *Anfione e Zeto*, 13, 2000, p. 71.

10 For a detailed analysis of Renzo Piano's sketches and their centrality in his planning method, see Claudia Conforti, Francesco Dal Co, *Renzo Piano. Gli schizzi*, Electa, Milan 2007.

11 Conversation between the author and Giorgio Bianchi, Genoa, 29 July 2020.

12 See Lorenzo Ciccarelli, 'Renzo Piano Building Workshop. Officina genovese, officina parigina', in *L'Industria delle Costruzioni*, 447, 2016, pp. 4–11.

13 Francesco Dal Co, 'La torre del New York Times', in F. Irace (ed.), *Renzo Piano Building Workshop. Le città visibili*. Triennale Electa, Milan 2007, pp. 65–69.

14 *The Shard*, Renzo Piano Foundation, Genoa 2012, p. 18.

15 A detail that was also highlighted by Chiara Calderini, 'Struttura e forma', in *Casabella*, 818, 2012, p. 80.

16 *The Shard*, op. cit., p. 56.

17 Alfredo Zappa, 'Trasparenze', in *Casabella*, 818, 2012, pp. 84–87.

18 See *Athens. Stavros Niarchos Cultural Center*, Renzo Piano Foundation, Genoa 2016; Federico Bucci, 'Nella luce dell'Attica, mentre ad Atene si spengono le luci', in *Casabella*, 865, 2016, pp. 62–81; Victoria Newhouse, *Chaos and Culture. Renzo Piano Building Workshop and the Stavros Niarchos Foundation Cultural Center in Athens*, The Monacelli Press, New York 2017.

19 Conversation between the author and Giorgio Bianchi, Genoa, 29 July 2020.

20 The opera house can accommodate up to 1,400 people. Alongside it is a 450-seater auditorium for drama productions and five rehearsal rooms for the orchestra, chorus and corps de ballet. The library, meanwhile, also has rooms for children's activities, recording studios and a business centre for training courses.

21 The wisdom of this decision is attested by the immediate success of the park and cultural centre. In its first three years it received more than 12 million visitors.

22 See Federico Bucci, 'RPBW: un brano di città intessuta con pietra maltese' in *Casabella*, 853, 2015, pp. 5–23.

23 Conversation between the author and Antonio Belvedere, 14 April 2021.

24 Vincenzo Sapienza, 'Opera House Ruins Theatre', in *Modulo*, 386, 2013, pp. 592–604.

25 Alessandro Clementi, Elio Piroddi, L'Aquila, Laterza, Rome-Bari 1986.

26 See Lorenzo Ciccarelli (ed.), *Renzo Piano, un auditorium per L'Aquila*, Textus, L'Aquila 2022.

27 The plan was drawn up by Renzo Piano and Paolo Colonna (RPBW) in collaboration with Atelier Traldi, Favero&Milan Ingegneria, Studio Franco Giorgetta for the landscaping, Müller-Bbm for the acoustics and Gae Engineering for fire prevention.

28 Conversation between the author and Alessandro Traldi, 11 November 2021.

29 Conversation between the author and Paolo Colonna, Paris, 3 December 2018.

30 Cesare Cattaneo, 'Edilizia industrializzata in legno "esercizio" tecnologico e architettonico', in *Il nuovo cantiere*, 1, 2013, pp. 24–29.

31 Piano had experimented with a similar use of colour for the prefabricated ceramic components of the facade of the Central St Giles in London, see Jean-Marie Martin, 'Un nuovo, vecchio isolato londinese, Saint Giles, Londra', in *Casabella*, 793, 2010, pp. 51–72.

32 On 27 June 2013 the L'Aquila Municipal Council decided to turn the auditorium into 'Casa Comunale' (town hall) as per Article 106 of the Civil Code, justifying their decision by citing the shortage of other availabe premises in the city.

33 See Lia Piano (ed.), *Emergency Children's Hospital*, Renzo Piano Foundation, Genoa 2021; Camillo Magni, 'Efficienza e terra cruda', in *Casabella*, 920, 2021, pp. 88–99.

34 See Francesca Serrazzanetti (ed.), *TAMassociati. Taking Care. Architetture con Emergency*, Electa, Milan 2017.

35 Input was also received from Studio Giorgetta for the landscaping, Milan Ingegneria for the structural engineering, and technicians from Mapei in developing the aggregates mixed with the raw earth used for the walls of the paediatric centre.

36 Conversation between the author and Giorgio Grandi, Genoa, 24 May 2021.

37 Elisa Portigliatti, 'Tradizione e innovazione: il pisé', in Lia Piano (ed.) 2021, op. cit., pp. 48–51.

PERSONAL AND COLLECTIVE: RECENT ACTIVITIES **223**

End matter

Since the 1960s Renzo Piano
and his colleagues have been
responsible for hundreds of
projects, which have been
discussed in countless publications.
Following the critical approach
adopted in this work, we have
also been selective regarding
biographical and project-related
information when drawing up the
chronology. Readers looking for
a fuller account of the RPBW's
projects should consult Piano's
*Giornale di bordo. Autobiografia
per progetti* (1966–2016).

CHRONOLOGY

1937

Renzo Piano is born in the Genoa suburb of Pegli.

1958–1964

University studies, first in Florence then at the Milan Polytechnic.

1970

Meeting in London with Richard Rogers, whom he partners in the Piano & Rogers practice.

1971

The Piano & Rogers practice, with Gianfranco Franchini and Ove Arup & Partners, wins the international competition to design the Pompidou Centre.

1977

Inauguration of the Pompidou Centre on 31 January. Piano dissolves his partnership with Rogers and returns to Genoa.

1978–1980

Piano forms a partnership with engineer Peter Rice, thus founding the Piano & Rice practice.

1981

Foundation of the Building Workshop, with offices in Genoa and Paris.

228

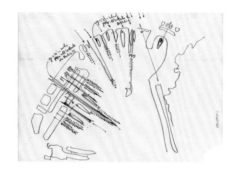

1981-1986

The Menil
Collection,
Houston.

1983-1984

Musical space
for *Prometeo*,
a work by
Luigi Nono.

1983-1986

Travelling
pavilion
for IBM.

1983-2003

Restructuring of
Fiat's Lingotto
factory in Turin.

1985-2001

Reclamation
of the Porto
Vecchio (Old
Harbour) area,
Genoa.

1987-1991

Residential
complex, Rue
de Meaux,
Paris.

1988-1994

1989-1991

1991-1998

Terminal
for Kansai
International
Airport,
Osaka.

Premises of
the Renzo
Piano Building
Workshop,
Punta Nave,
Genoa.

Jean-Marie
Tjibaou
Cultural
Centre,
Nouméa, New
Caledonia.

1991–2000

Museum for
the Beyeler
Foundation,
Basel.

1992–2000

Reconstruction
of the
Potsdamer
Platz area,
Berlin.

1994–2002

Parco della
Musica
Auditorium,
Rome.

1998

Awarded
the Pritzker
Prize.

1999–2003

Nasher
Sculpture
Center,
Dallas.

1999–2005

Extension
to the High
Museum of
Art, Atlanta.

1999–2005

Zentrum Paul Klee, Bern.

2000–2006

Refurbishment and extension of the Morgan Library, New York.

2000–2007

New premises for the New York Times, New York.

2000–2008

New premises for the California Academy of Sciences, San Francisco.

2000–2009

Extension to the Art Institute of Chicago.

2000–2012

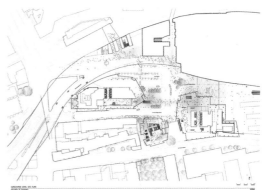

London Bridge Tower (The Shard), Europe's highest skyscraper, London.

2002–2016

Science museum and Le Albere district, Trento.

2004

Renzo Piano Foundation constituted in Genoa.

2005–2012

Extension to the Isabella Stewart Gardner Museum, Boston.

2006–2011

Convent of St Clare and visitor centre for the Chapel of Notre-Dame du Haut, Ronchamp.

2006–2012

Astrup Fearnley Museum of Modern Art, Oslo.

2006–2014

Headquarters of the Fondation Pathé, Paris.

2006–2014

Refurbishment and extension of the Harvard Art Museum, Cambridge, Massachusetts.

2007–2013

Extension to the Kimbell Art Museum, Fort Worth.

2007-2015

New premises
for the
Whitney
Museum of
American Art,
New York.

2008-2016

Stavros
Niarchos
Foundation
Cultural
Centre,
Athens.

2009-2015

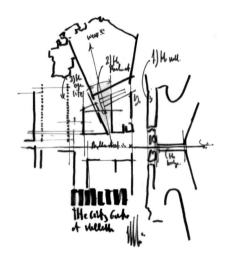

City Gate, new
Parliament
building and
Opera House,
Valletta.

2010–2012

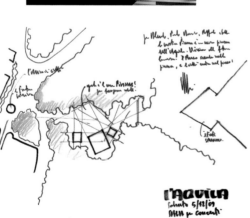

Auditorium del Parco, L'Aquila, Italy.

2010–2017

New premises for the Palais de Justice and Tribunal de Paris, Porte de Clichy, Paris.

2012–2021

Academy Museum of Motion Pictures, Los Angeles.

2013

Giorgio Napolitano, President of the Italian Republic, appoints Renzo Piano senator for life.

2013–2020

Children's Surgical Hospital, Entebbe, Uganda, for NGO EMERGENCY.

2014–2020

Campus for the École Normale Supérieure, Paris-Saclay.

2015–2021

Transformation of old Moscow power station into the GES-2 Cultural Centre.

2016–2022

New premises for the Istanbul Modern Museum.

2018–2020

Planning and construction of the San Giorgio Bridge in Genoa to replace the old Morandi Viaduct, which collapsed with tragic results on 14 August 2018.

Ongoing projects: Stavros Niarchos Foundation Agora Institute at Johns Hopkins University, Baltimore; hospital centres, financed by the Stavros Niarchos Foundation, in the Greek cities of Komotini, Thessaloniki and Sparta; Science Gateway Building at CERN in Geneva; new Palace of Justice, Toronto; paediatric hospice in Bologna; and ISMETT 2 hospital in Palermo.

BIBLIOGRAPHY

M. Zanuso, R. Piano, R. Lucci, *Elementi di tecnologia dei materiali come introduzione allo studio del design*, Milan 1967.

R. Piano, M. Arduino, M. Fazio, *Antico è bello. Il recupero della città*, Rome-Bari 1980.

Renzo Piano. *Pezzo per pezzo*, ed. G. Donin, Rome 1982.

M. Dini, Renzo Piano. *Progetti e architetture 1964–1983*, Milan 1983.

R. Piano, *Dialoghi di cantiere*, Rome-Bari 1986.

R. Piano, R. Rogers, *Du Plateau Beaubourg au Centre Georges Pompidou*, Paris 1987.

R. Banham, 'In the Neighborhood of Art', in *Art in America*, 6, 1987, pp. 124–129.

R. Banham, 'Making Architecture. The High Craft of Renzo Piano', in *Renzo Piano Building Workshop 1964–1988*, Tokyo 1989, pp. 151–158.

P. Goldberger, Renzo Piano. *Buildings and Projects 1971–1989*, New York 1989.

P. Buchanan, *Renzo Piano Building Workshop. Complete Works*, London 1993–2008.

N. Silver, *The Making of Beaubourg*, Cambridge (MA) 1994.

P. Rice, *An Engineer Imagines*, London 1994.

Kansai International Airport Passenger Terminal Building, monographic edition of *Japan Architect*, 15, 1994.

Renzo Piano, 'Il mestiere più antico del mondo', in *Micromega*, 2, 1996, pp. 107–120.

Renzo Piano, *Un regard construit*, ed. O. Cinqualbre, Paris 2000.

C. Conforti, F. Dal Co, Renzo Piano. *Gli schizzi*, Milan 2007.

Renzo Piano Building Workshop. *Le città visibili*, ed. F. Irace, Milan 2007.

The Menil Collection, Genoa 2007.

Fondation Beyeler, Genoa 2008.

Centre Culturel Jean-Marie Tjibaou, Genoa 2009.

California Academy of Sciences, Genoa 2010.

'Being Renzo Piano', monographic issue of *Abitare* 497, 2009.

R. Piano, *La responsabilità dell'architetto*, Bagno a Ripoli 2010.

The Shard. London Bridge Quarter, Genoa 2012.

F. Dal Co, *Renzo Piano*, Milan 2014.

Ronchamp Monastery, Genoa 2014.

Whitney Museum of American Art, Genoa 2015.

Renzo Piano Building Workshop. Progetti d'acqua, Genoa 2015.

C. Conforti, 'Renzo Piano, un architecte à l'écoute de la ville', in *ArtItalies*, 21, 2015, pp. 145–151.

Stavros Niarchos Cultural Center, Genoa 2016.

Centre Pompidou, Genoa 2017.

L. Ciccarelli, *Renzo Piano prima di Renzo Piano. I maestri e gli esordi*, Macerata 2017.

R. Piano, *Giornale di bordo. Autobiografia per progetti 1966–2016*, Genoa 2017.

Centro Botín, Genoa 2018.

Renzo Piano. *The Art of Making Buildings*, London 2018.

Ponte Genova San Giorgio, Genoa 2020.

E. Stach, *Renzo Piano Building Workshop. Space-Detail-Light*, Basel 2021.

Emergency Children's Hospital, Genoa 2021.

S. Russo Ermolli, G. Galluccio, *Materia, Prodotto, Dato. Il valore dell'informazione nelle architetture del Renzo Piano Building Workshop*, Sant'Arcangelo di Romagna 2021.

INDEX OF PROPER AND GEOGRAPHICAL NAMES

238

CREDITS FOR PROJECTS AND ICONOGRAPHIC REFERENCES

1964–1965
Reinforced Polyester Space Frames
Genoa, Italy
Studio Piano

1965
Woodworking Shop
Ceranesi (Genoa), Italy
Client: Falegnameria Mazzitelli
Studio Piano

1966–1968
Prestressed Steel and Reinforced Polyester
    Structure
Genoa, Italy
Client: Impresa Piano Ermanno
Studio Piano

1968–1969
The Renzo Piano office
Genoa, Italy
Studio Piano

1971–1977
Centre Georges Pompidou
Paris, France
Client: Ministry of Cultural Affairs, Ministry of
    National Education
Piano & Rogers practice, architects

1978–1980
Fiat VSS experimental car
Client: Fiat Auto S.p.A., IDEA Institute
Piano & Rice practice

1979
Habitat Television Programme
Client: RAI (Radiotelevisione Italiana)
Piano & Rice practice

1978–1982
EH, Evolutive Housing
Corciano (Perugia), Italy
Client: Vibrocemento Perugia S.p.A.
Studio Piano & Rice

1979
Otranto Urban Regeneration Workshop
Otranto, Italy
Client: UNESCO (S. Busutill,
    W. Tochtermann)
Studio Piano & Rice

1981–1987
The Menil Collection
Houston (Texas), USA
Client: The Menil Foundation
Piano & Fitzgerald, architects

1988–1994
Kansai International Airport Passenger
    Terminal Building
Osaka, Japan
Client: Kansai International Airport Co. Ltd.
Renzo Piano Building Workshop, architects
    – N. Okabe, senior partner in charge,
    in association with Nikken Sekkei
    Ltd., Aéroports de Paris, Japan Airport
    Consultants Inc.

1992–2000
Potsdamer Platz
Berlin, Germany
Client: Daimler-Chrysler AG
Renzo Piano Building Workshop architects
    in association with Christoph Kohlbecker
    (Gaggenau)

1985–2001
Redevelopment of Genoa's Porto Vecchio
Genoa, Italy
Client: City of Genoa + Porto Antico SpA
Renzo Piano Building Workshop, architects

1999–2005
High Museum of Art Expansion
Atlanta (Georgia), USA
Client: High Museum of Art + Woodruff Arts
    Center
Renzo Piano Building Workshop in
    collaboration with Lord, Aeck & Sargent
    Inc. (Atlanta), architects

2000–2006
Renovation and expansion of Morgan Library
New York, USA
Client: The Morgan Library
Renzo Piano Building Workshop
in collaboration with Beyer Blinder Belle LLP
    (New York), architects

2000–2012
The Shard – London Bridge Tower
London, UK
Client: Sellar Property Group
Renzo Piano Building Workshop architects
    in collaboration with Adamson Associates
    (Toronto, London)

2008–2016
Stavros Niarchos Foundation Cultural Centre
Athens, Greece
Client: The Stavros Niarchos Foundation
Renzo Piano Building Workshop architects
    in collaboration with Betaplan (Athens)

2009–2015
Valletta City Gate
Valletta, Malta
Client: Grand Harbour Regeneration
    Corporation
Renzo Piano Building Workshop architects
    in collaboration with Architecture Project
    (Valletta)

2010–2012
Auditorium del Parco
L'Aquila, Italy
Client: Provincia Autonoma di Trento
Renzo Piano Building Workshop, architects
    in collaboration with Atelier Traldi (Milan)

2013–2020
Children's Surgical Hospital, Entebbe,
    Uganda
Client: EMERGENCY
Renzo Piano Building Workshop & Studio
    TAMassociati, architects

© Gianni Berengo Gardin / Contrasto: 11, 15,
    16a, 72–73, 75, 76, 91, 92, 94, 133.
© Will Boase / Archivio Emergency (used
    with permission): 216–217, 220–221.
© Marco Caselli Nirmal (with permission):
    210–211, 234a.
© Centre Pompidou (with permission): 69a.
© Michel Denancé: 19, 20–21, 22–23, 70, 74,
    144–145, 146, 152–153, 155, 161, 162, 163, 164–
    165, 171, 172–173, 176–177, 178, 184a, 186, 191,
    193, 194–195, 198–199, 200, 202, 203, 233bd.
© Dennis Gilbert / Viewpictures: 129.
© Chris Martin: 182–183.
© Jacques Minassian (with permission): 8–9.
© Rogers Stirk Harbour + Partners © Arup
    (with permission): 6.
© Courtney Robbins (with permission):
    222b.
© Ruby on Thursdays (with permission): 192.
© Stavros Niarchos Foundation Cultural
    Center (with permission): 233c.
© Rob Telford: 185.

© Renzo Piano Foundation: 1, 3, 4, 5, 9, 10,
12-13, 14, 40, 41, 42, 44S, 44d, 45, 47, 48a,
48c, 48b, 49, 50b, 52, 53s, 53d, 54s, 55, 56,
58a, 58b, 59, 78-79, 80, 82a, 82b, 83a, 85a,
85b, 86–87, 87b, 88, 89a, 89b, 90s, 90d, 93,
97, 100s, 100d, 100–101, 103b, 106–107, 122a,
122c, 148–149, 228ad, 229cs, 233as, 233cd;
photographs Richard T. Bryant Photographe,
98, 111, 113; photographs David Crossley,
102s, 102d; photographs Stefano Goldberg
16b, 17, 24–25, 26, 27b, 29; photographs
Paul Hester, 96–97, 104–105, 228as;
photographs Hickey & Robertson
Photography, 108, 110, 114–115; photographs
Shunji Ishida, 83b, 87a, 103a; photograph
Shinkenchiku-sha Co. Ltd., 128; photograph
Deidi von Schaewen, 112.
© Fondazione Renzo Piano © Rogers Stirk
    Harbour + Partners (with permission):
    7, 62, 62–63, 64, 66, 67, 68, 68–69, 69b, 71.
© Renzo Piano Foundation © Studio Piano:
    50as, 50ad, 51as, 51ad, 51b, 57as, 57ad,
    57bs, 57bd.
© Renzo Piano: 132a, 132b, 149s, 149d, 158,
    167, 176, 188, 189, 196, 197, 204, 212, 213, 225,
    230c, 234b, 235a.
© Renzo Piano Building Workshop:
    18, 84, 118, 122-123, 123A, 135, 144,
    156–157, 159, 166, 169, 180–181, 184B, 190,
    206–207, 208, 214–215, 231b; photograph
    Atelier Traldi – Alessandro Traldi
    Architetto, 209; photograph Richard
    Cadan, 168; photographs Enrico Cano,
    136–137, 224–225, 230a, 235c, 235b
    (1–3); photographs Stefano Goldberg,
    27a, 232; photograph Yoshio Hata, 125;
    photographs Kanji Hiwatashi, 118–119,
    130–131; photograph Alistar Hunter, 229bd;
    photographs Shunji Ishida, 126–127, 127;
    photographs Yutaka Kinumaki, 120, 229bs;
    photographs Nic Lehoux, 233cs, 233bs;
    photographs William Matthews, 187,
    231b; photographs Vincent Mosch, 134,
    138–139, 140–141; photographs Emmanuel
    Museruka – Malaika Mediafoto, 218–219,
    222a; photographs Stefano Percivale 227a,
    227b, 230b; photographs Publifoto, Genoa,
    150–151, 154, 228c, 228b, 229ad.
© Renzo Piano Building Workshop
© Agence de Développement de la Culture
    Kanak (ADCK): photograph John Gollings,
    229cd; photograph Pierre-Alain Pantz,
    229bd.